Positively Brentford

A Pictorial History of Brentford FC 1896 to 1996

Dan Jackson

DAN JACKSON
&
POLAR PUBLISHING

This book is dedicated to; my ever-supportive family, and "Bernie Slaven" in particular, who has more than succeeded in passing on to me his obsession with the Bees; to the late Eric White, who would, I hope, have enjoyed this book so much; and above all, to Brentford fans - not vast in number, but on their day passionate, committed, and fiercely loyal at a time when it's all too easy to follow the Manchester United's of this world.

Acknowledgments

Because it's taken me such a hideously long time to finish this project, a large number of good folk have inevitably become involved to some degree along the way in helping me overcome the many obstacles that I've faced. I'd like to thank them all (or at least all those that I can remember), so if you're not too interested in a who's who of those that have contributed to this masterpiece, don't bother reading the following bit - it's really dull, rather like a visit to Craven Cottage.

Thanks to Julian Baskcomb and all the team at Polar who were prepared to take the gamble (you'll get the money one day, honest); to Clever Trev, the graphic designer; to Dennis Turner for the wise advice when I knew nothing (sorry about the Fulham gag - it's in the blood!); to Eileen and David White, who were kind enough to help during a time of great personal adversity; to Paul Lamond, who provided much encouragement and advice; to Graham Haynes, who got me out of a tight spot on more than one occasion; to Ian Westbrook, who helped as much as possible whenever I asked for contacts or information; to Greville Waterman for the financial advice and sponsorship deal; to those nice men at Ericsson Ltd; to Peter Gilham for the 'behind-the-scenes' help at Brentford; to Lee Doyle for providing me with a multitude of top shots; to Robin Pearson for the genuine interest and ripping photos; to Dave Lane for the plugs - who said fanzine editors are nothing but bad news?; to Chris Hatherall, who happily left me to ravage the Ealing Gazette photo files (unlike another paper's staff); to Neil Chippendale at Hounslow Library - a learned Brentford fan, would you believe; to Bill Vose for the sturdy camera work; to Jim Tinkler, a man with more Bees memories than you've had hot dinners; to Matty Verkamman - a Bee with clogs, no doubt; to Ron Lewis at the Middlesex Chronicle; to Ron Saunders (no, not that Ron Saunders) at British Pathe News - cheap, and very cheerful; to Christine Bell at the Bolton Evening News; to Sheila Ballantyne at the Southern Daily Echo; to the Valiant Tom Morris; to Adam Scott - great photos - you'll go far, my son; to Dick Rattray for the 1960's pics; to David Downs for the Reading photos; to David Ticehurst for the old postcards; to the "staff" at Sportspages, even though they have yet to bow to the ultimately undeniable fact that Griffin Park is the true home of football; and to anyone else that has responded positively to the misfortune of being contacted by me over the last three years.

First published in Great Britain 1997 by Dan Jackson
in association with
Polar Print Group Ltd
2, Uxbridge Road, Leicester LE4 7ST
England

ISBN 1 899538 02 X

Designed and Printed by
Polar Print Group Ltd
2, Uxbridge Road, Leicester LE4 7ST
Tel: (0116) 261 0800

Photographs are courtesy of:
The Press Association, Lee Doyle, Reed Northern Newspapers, Hulton-Getty Collection, Eric White family, Ealing Gazette, Middlesex Chronicle, Brentford & Chiswick Times, Mrs H.A. Redgrave, Nottingham Post, Wolverhampton Express & Star, Bolton Evening News, Dave Lane, Oldham Chronicle, Topham Picture Source, British Pathe News, Tom Morris, Adam Scott, David Downs, David Ticehurst, Robin Pearson & Keith Warren.
Most remaining photographs are from the private collection of the author or from albums owned by supporters or former players. We have been unable to trace the sources of all these pictures, but any photographer involved is cordially invited to contact the publishers in writing providing proof of copyright.

CONTENTS

"Like many, I was first taken to a football match by my father. Unlike most, however, neither of us remember the occasion or the result, although chances are that Brentford probably lost."

I originally intended to start the introduction with the above sentence, because in many ways it seemed to encapsulate much of the gut-wrenching despair and disbelief caused by a multitude of last-minute defeats at the hands of those both worthy and unworthy. However, while supporting Brentford may have had an adverse effect on my health and hairline, when I think back beyond the anguish and tedium (which, after all, are emotions universal to all football fans from Brentford to Barcelona), there they are - the good bits.

For myself, these start with flashes of McCulloch, Sweetzer and Phillips scoring almost at will during the late 1970's, but while our youngest fans may even have trouble recalling the exploits of the 1991/92 promotion team, each generation will hold dear memories of their childhood heroes taking the field at Griffin Park. This being so, while one aim of this book is to provide us all with a permanent reminder of players and matches we have known and loved (or not, as the case may be), the other is to bring to life characters and games that we cannot recall.

Unfortunately, having never won any major competition of note has its drawbacks, and seldom has the media eye been focused on events at Griffin Park. Naturally the local press have been taking snaps from the touchlines since photographic reproduction in mass-circulation newspapers became widespread in the late 1920's, but papers have come and gone, and whole archives have either been lost or destroyed. No trace, for example, could be found of any prints from the County of Middlesex Independent, which covered the Bees' "glory years" in great detail, or from the Slough Evening Mail, which gave much space to Brentford during the 1970's and early 1980's.

Consequently I have had to include a number of lower-quality newspaper cuttings to cover the period prior to about 1935, while there are also a few 'gaps', for example from the Francis-Towers era of the late 1950's, that proved impossible to fill. However, I hope you will agree that these complications have not taken too much away from a book compiled to make you proud to be a Bee!

Before I started any research for this book, Patsy Hendren, Bill Lane, Jack Holliday, Dai Hopkins, Ken Coote, Jim Towers, John O'Mara and others were mere names and statistics, often mentioned with reverence by others but never truly reflected upon. The following photographs will hopefully allow you, as they did me, access to these names and many more. Moreover, I would like to think that the book acts as something of a social history, helping to chronicle the link between the Club and its fans and enabling us to travel back to the Southern League days of flat caps, shirts and ties, to the Thirties and Forties, when thirty thousand or more regularly filled Griffin Park to see the rising stars of London football in action, through to the supporters' actions during the 1967 takeover crisis, to the 70's with sideburns and flares, and beyond.

Indeed, the two great constants through the history of Brentford F.C. and through this book have been the supporters and Griffin Park itself, but while it is wonderous to look back on the old New Road and Brook Road terraces, heaving with thousands of screaming fans, the ground has changed almost beyond recognition in the last decade. As the Club recovers from its late 1960's and 1970's struggles against takeover, bankruptcy and re-election, it may perhaps be time to look for pastures new, but one thing is for certain; the tradition and history of Brentford F.C. and Griffin Park will never be forgotten.

Dan Jackson, October 1996

DAN JACKSON

The day after Dan Jackson was born in London in 1969, Brentford drew 0-0 with Wrexham at Griffin Park. He did not know it at the time, but research into the pictorial history of this west London football club was going to occupy a depressingly large chunk of his early adult life. In due course he graduated in Politics and International Relations at Sheffield and Nottingham Universities. This knowledge of international warfare, unarmed combat and political in-fighting provided the ideal background for a job specialising in football publications in a sports bookstore. In response to the unrelenting demand for books about the Bees, he initiated the 'Positively Brentford' project.

Dan works at Sportspages Bookshop and lives in an unfashionable part of north west London. His hobbies include pouring scorn on 'supporters' of top Premiership clubs, and ranting inanely on the relative merit of obscure football attendance figures.

Dan Jackson's first appearance in a Brentford shirt!

Keith Westcott, Director of Ericsson Mobile Terminals

THE old saying goes that a picture is worth a thousand words, but in 'Positively Brentford' Brentford fans will be able to enjoy the best of all possible worlds, with hundreds of archive photographs accompanied by descriptive captions and original newspaper reports all guaranteed to stir the memories.

The history of Brentford Football Club is a long and honourable one punctuated with landmarks such as the War Cup Final victory over Portsmouth, regular wins over our old rivals, Arsenal, in the First Division, and in more recent times, the appearance at Wembley in the Freight Rover Cup Final and the amazing run to the Sixth Round of the FA Cup in 1989.

Great players have graced Griffin Park over the years and the images in 'Positively Brentford' will enable you to pick out your favourites, wallow once more in the memories and dream of what was and what might have been.

Ericsson Mobile Phones is delighted to be the sponsor of a club which not only has such a proud heritage, but also much to be optimistic about in the future. Our involvement with the club has helped us solidify our position in the Premier League of mobile phone manufacturers and we look forward to joint success over the next few years of our partnership.

'Positively Brentford' has truly been a labour of love for Dan Jackson, and his enthusiasm and detective work has uncovered many photographs that were previously thought lost for ever.

Ericsson are proud to have supported Dan Jackson's endeavours and I hope that you enjoy 'Positively Brentford' as much as I have.

Keith Westcott, *Director of Ericsson Mobile Terminals*

THIS project, which has been a number of years in the making, is the perfect companion to the excellent '100 Years of Brentford' published in 1989. It is the result of many hundreds of painstaking hours of research, covering the length and breadth of Great Britain by Bees fan Dan Jackson.

It is a pictorial testament to the many hundreds, maybe thousands, of players who have worn the colours of Brentford Football Football and others who have served the Club in various capacities, over the years.

Whilst the Club, in the eyes of some, may not have enjoyed the success achieved by some of its supposedly more illustrious London neighbours, it has certainly a history of which to be proud. And it is through these pages that the reader will be able to recapture and relive those special memories oft spoken of by our predecessors, and indeed a good many that, thanks to meticulous research, will now spring to life.

Memories, both young and old, will be stirred, for there is no better way to enjoy the emotions and passions of times gone by, than through the camera lens.

Peter Gilham, *Marketing Manager Brentford Football Club*

Street urchins loiter outside John Grew's Fried Fish Shop at 17 Half Acre in Brentford, perhaps waiting for their stewed eels and mashed potatoes. The advertisement on the door to the left is for the Bees' game against 2nd Grenadier Guards, played on February 29th 1896 at Shotters Field, the result of which is unknown.

January 1905. *The roof of the recently erected main stand lies scattered over a number of damaged houses on Braemar Road following a particularly ferocious winter storm, justifying the fears of the borough surveyor who had adjudged the stand and dressing room to be unsafe. It was in this state of disrepair that Griffin Park accommodated the biggest ever crowd to watch a Brentford match to that date (17,500) as the Bees played host to Reading in the intermediate round of the FA Cup on 14th January.*

3rd December 1904. Southampton beat Brentford 1-0 at Griffin Park in what was the club's first season at their new home.

The photos (above) offer an excellent view of the Braemar Road stand, a combination of the stand taken from the previous ground at Boston Park Cricket Club together with a newly built extension, which allowed the capacity on that side of the ground to be raised from 800 to 1500. Note also that the players appear to be 'coloured in', a commonly used technique at a time when photographic reproduction was not considered to be of a quality high enough to provide the required definition.

Four portraits from the 1906/07 season.

*Left to right... Forward **Pat Hagan**, acquired from Hibernian... **Tommy Shanks**, centre forward and Irish international... **Charlie Williams**, the first ever keeper to score directly from a goal kick... Winger **Freddy Pentland**, who was to be capped four times for England. Later in life, Pentland was held prisoner of war in Germany during the First World War, and went on to be involved with the formation of Athletic Bilbao in Spain (who play in red and white stripes...).*

January 14th 1911.
The draw of First Division Preston North End as opponents in the first round of the FA Cup guaranteed Brentford's second five figure gate in three weeks. 14,000 fans cheered on the Bees, but to no avail as the League side won through thanks to a fortuitous penalty decision by the referee, as described by the County of Middlesex Independent:

January 1st 1910.
Brentford's best crowd of the season (12,000) saw the team sustain only their second home defeat of the season, losing 1-0 to a lucky QPR side in a rather ragged game spoiled by the already fierce rivalry between the two teams.

Top: 'Dusty' Rhodes clears for Brentford.

Right: Rangers' keeper saves from Rushton (left) and Reid.

Below: Midfield headwork.

"Preston can account themselves lucky to figure in the second round in the Cup competition at least without another game being necessary. Of the two sides, the visiting team was the weaker and yet they ran out victorious by a goal scored from a penalty, to nil. Let it be admitted that Kennedy did accidently handle in the penalty area some seven minutes from the start, but the infringement scarcely merited the infliction of the full punishment, especially having regard to the fact that on two or three other occasions Brentford should have been (but were not) awarded penalty kicks for offences quite deliberate and far more serious. Brentford have suffered two or three times this year from poor refereeing, but on no occasion has the presiding official of the game proved so seriously at fault as on Saturday. One does not want to be harsh, and it can only be assumed that the gentleman in charge was not up to the mark and had a day off in consequence.

"Of the players, no one can raise a word in criticism of the defence which did all that was necessary on every occasion. It was in the front line that we failed. Reid was too well watched to be able to do anything, but he managed to give chances to others, which were not taken full advantage of."

68   LOTINGA'S WEEKLY.   JANUARY 28TH, 1911.

How Preston North End "knocked out" Brentford in the Cup's First Round!

With a view of the fateful penalty-kick which decided the match in favour of the First League team.

1. The full-back, Rodway, about to take advantage of the full limit of football law, namely, the disturbing and deciding penalty-kick awarded by the referee for "hands" by a Brentford defender within the penalty area.

2. Of all the thousands of spectators none watched the game with keener interest than the trainers of the opposing teams, T. Cowper (Brentford) and J. R. Clayton (Preston North End) who are here shown.

3. The toss-up for choice of ends; to the left, the North End's veteran goalkeeping captain, McBride; in the centre, Mr. Pearson, the referee; to the right, Rhodes, the Brentford skipper.

4. A section of the crowd around by the Brentford F.C.'s Supporters' League quarters with two heads ringed out to denote that their owners can claim a guinea each from this paper.

5. McBride "makes a basket" of himself by snapping up a straight hot shot.

6. The winning team, the present-day representatives of what was once known as "Proud Preston, or the team of all the talents."

7. Ling, the Brentford goalie, making as speedy a clearance as possible to avoid the centre-forward's rush.

JANUARY 6, 1912.   LOTINGA'S WEEKLY.   997

Brentford and Crystal Palace.

Scenes in the Southern League game at Griffin Park, Brentford, which resulted in a win for the home team by one goal to nothing.

EXCLUSIVE PICTURES from OWN PHOTOGRAPHERS.

1. Brentford kick off on a soft, slippery pitch.

2. One of the outstanding features of the match was the goalkeeping of Johnson, the Crystal Palace custodian, his brilliant saves causing great enthusiasm. The picture shows him on the ground, after stopping a hot shot, which Rippon, from the rebound, attempted to head through. Johnson, however, was up in time, and again saved.

3 and 5. The Brentford team, who at present occupy rather a lowly position in the Southern League table.

4. The toss-up. On the left: Hughes, the Crystal Palace captain; in the centre, Mr. H. E. Bamlett (the referee), and Rhodes, the Brentford skipper.

We publish a portion of the rather too enthusiastic spectators (at least, the referee appeared to think so), who gave vocal assistance towards Brentford's victory. Three of them are ringed for our "Dollar" prize.

Read our new joint football plans between " John Bull " and " Lotinga's Weekly."

April 14th 1911. Brighton scored the only goal of the match as the Bees travelled down to Hove for this Southern League First Division match.

Above: One spectator gets carried away by the prospect of the match and attempts to tackle a corner flag as the perplexed crowd look on.

December 23rd 1911. Brentford, struggling at the wrong end of the table, eased their relegation concerns with a one goal to nil victory over local rivals Crystal Palace in front of 5,000 spectators.

Left: Various scenes at the match as seen by the photographer of "Lotinga's Weekly", an early sporting periodical. Note the reference to Brentford's "rather too enthusiastic spectators" - perhaps an excessive brandishing of early Chomp bars or cheese?

LOTINGA'S WEEKLY.

How Crystal Palace beat Brentford.

The replayed tie on the Sydenham ground resulted in a very easy win for the Palace, who thus qualify to meet Sunderland in the second round of the Cup.

1. Some of the nine thousand spectators who braved the wintery weather to see the Palace win by 4 goals to nil.

2. Smith, who played such a brilliant game for the Palace at centre-forward.

3. Smith scoring the first goal of the match. He shot hard and the ball striking Spratt, the Brentford back, it passed through the goal, the goalkeeper having no chance to save.

4. Hughes (Crystal Palace) and Rhodes (Brentford) shake hands before spinning the coin.

January 17th 1912. Having defeated the First Battalion King's Royal Rifles and Southend United in the qualifying rounds, Brentford made the first round proper of the FA Cup, only to play Crystal Palace again. This time, however, the league result did not repeat itself, and having drawn 0-0 at Griffin Park the south London team won through easily, thrashing a Brentford team depleted by injury 4-0 at their Sydenham ground.

29th January 1927. Having dismissed Clapton, Gillingham and Oldham Athletic in the previous rounds of the FA Cup campaign (all after replays), Brentford, under the stewardship of new manager Harry Curtis, found themselves drawn out of the hat against First Division West Ham. Sensing the possibility of a cross-town giantkilling, the fixture was the centre of much media attention and drew a huge crowd. The game was a classic cup tie.

Above: The Bees defend their goal.

Below: Brentford's keeper Ferguson saves on the goal line as (l-r) Butler, Donnelly and Watkins look on.

Brentford's goal was described thus:

"The ball came in with deadly accuracy from the foot of Patsy to the head of Lane, who deflected it into the corner of the net, well out of Hufton's reach. And what a roar went up; the Bees' supporters yelled themselves hoarse, and loudly clamoured for more."

"Not one of the 40,000 spectators who, between them, paid £2,780 to witness the match, had a dull moment during the hour and a half that the struggle lasted.

"The conditions were not conducive to good football. There was no rain, snow, sleet, or inconveniences of that kind, but otherwise it was the very reverse of pleasant. There was a wild, gusty wind blowing, edged with ice, it seemed, as one waited for the appearance of the rival teams in the arena, and it was this wind that Brentford had to face in the first half.

"From the start Brentford made it plain that they did not intend to allow West Ham to develop the game on the lines they would have liked. The Hammers sought to exploit clever passing movements, and to finesse. In any event they would have found it difficult to do much of this on such a pitch, but with Brentford determined to play traditional Cup-tie football....chasing relentlessly and shooting as hard and often as possible, such a policy was foredoomed to failure. Brentford bustled with their work wholeheartedly,...and in the end were a trifle unfortunate not to have seized the victory.

"'Hit 'em and 'old 'em' was the war-cry of the several thousand Brentford enthusiasts who accompanied the team to Upton Park,...and the slogan - probably emanating from the Bees' great performance at Oldham - was manfully carried out by the Bees, for, after being a goal down in the first half, they hit back in the second half with a goal by Lane, and then proceeded to carry out the last part of the slogan - hold them.

(County of Middlesex Independent,
2nd February 1927)

Having held out for the draw, 20,799 turned up at Griffin Park the following Tuesday for the replay. To the delight of the home supporters, goals from Lane and Allen sealed an unexpected 2-1 victory over the Hammers, and secured Brentford's place in the draw for the 5th round, this time against Reading at Elm Park.

Brentford's cup run ended here, losing through a single first half goal from Reading's inside left Richardson, but the Bees' second local Cup derby in succession again proved to be of huge interest to the populace of Middlesex and Berkshire, and the crowd of 33,042 remains the largest ever at Elm Park to this day. Bees fans turned up at the ground in their hordes, as described in the local paper:

Above: A save by Ferguson, who played a fine game in the Brentford goal.

Right: Reading put one just outside the post.

Below right: Donnelly, unseen by the referee, keeps the ball out of the Bees' net with his hand.

"There were early indications of a big gate, and before 2.20 there must have been 18,000 present. And still there were crowds on the way. A quarter of an hour before the kick-off it seemed doubtful whether all would get in. It was a wonderful sight - with the ground packed. A large number of Brentford supporters travelled by chars-a-bancs, lorry and motor-car, [and they] early made a stir in Reading...it is a long while since so many supporters of a visiting club have been on Elm Park. Just how many supporters Brentford numbered it is difficult to say, but they must have run into thousands. They did not forget to let themselves be heard either, and Brentford were certainly at little disadvantage in the matter of vocal support. A section of them made themselves conspicuous with flags, bells, rattles and profuse decorations, and they had a song which embraced the names of the clubs which they had ousted from the FA competition. The Reading Temperance Band were in attendance an hour before the kick-off, and they played many of the songs which have been revived in the community singing campaign, [while] the Brentford contingent near the clock were amusing themselves with swaying to and fro with the music. "

(Berkshire Football Chronicle, February 19th 1927)

The players prepared for the tie at Reading by "taking the ozone and hot sea-baths" at Southend! Here, some of the team (left to right: Watkins, Lane, Ratcliffe (trainer), Douglas and Noble) enjoy a quiet game of solo.

September 7th 1929.
With three new proven
forwards (the
formidable Bill Lane
together with Cyril
Blackmore and Jackie
Foster) leading their
attack, the Bees had
begun their 1929/30
campaign by scoring six
goals in their first two
games against Swindon
Town and Clapton
Orient. In their next
match against Plymouth
Argyle at Home Park,
Bill Lane gave Brentford
the lead, only for the
home team to scramble
a point in the last
minute.

*The Bees' right back
Stevenson challenges for
the ball. Note that Argyle
had a black player on
their books (Leslie) - a
rarity in pre-War football.*

January 4th 1930. One of the most important games of the 1929/30 Third Division (South) season took place on this day at Griffin Park. Brentford and Plymouth Argyle were neck-and-neck in the race for the championship; leaders Argyle had only been beaten once all season, while the Bees, hot on their heels, were unbeaten at home.

A new attendance record was set as 22,000 crammed onto the terraces, and the majority went home happy as the Bees demolished their rivals, scoring in the first minute and adding another two without reply in the second period.

Below: Bill Lane, watched by Jack Lane, lunges forward in an attempt to intercept a hefty clearance by Plymouth's keeper Craig.

March 8th 1930. Having scored ten goals in their last two home games, putting five past both Watford and Fulham, the Bees kept up their promotion push and carried through their magnificent home form to dispose of another local team, Crystal Palace. Lane and Payne scored without reply much to pleasure of most of the 21,000 present.

Come the end of the season Brentford had scored 94 goals, losing only nine league matches and winning every one of their 21 home games, the latter a truly remarkable feat yet to be equalled by any other team. These nine defeats, however, were enough to edge Plymouth the title and promotion, denying the impressive Bees a chance to prove themselves in a higher division for a short while longer.

Left: Palace clear their area from a Brentford corner.

The record-breaking 1929-30 team.

Back row (left to right): R.Davis, R.Kane (trainer), G.Dumbrell, F.Fox, W.Hodge, J.Foster, H.Salt.
Front: D.Sherlaw, J.Lane, W.Lane, C.Blakemore, J.Payne, J.Bain.

12th December 1931.
The Bees had defeated Tunbridge Wells Rangers of the Southern League in the first round of the FA Cup, albeit only after a replay, and had drawn Norwich City in the second round at home. There was some cause for concern, as the East Anglians had been the only team to leave Griffin Park with either a win or a draw all season, but the sceptics were happily proved wrong as the Bees clipped the Canaries' wings, winning 4-1 and progressing to the third round.

Right: The Canaries' defence break up a Brentford raid.

Billy Lane (pictured here in his Spurs shirt), one of the Bees' finest ever strikers who scored an astonishing 84 goals in 114 appearances for the club. At the end of the 1931/32 season, the Bees were forced to sell Billy to Watford, against his will, in order to help fund the transfer of Jack Holliday, Billy Scott and Bert Watson from Middlesbrough, all three of whom played an integral part in Brentford's subsequent meteoric rise to the First Division.

BRITISH LEGION (Brentford Branch,)

A Comic Football Match
TOP HATS
v.
BONNETS

Will be held on the ground of the Brentford Football Club, at
GRIFFIN PARK

Braemar Road, Brentford, (by kind permission of the Directors),

On Easter Tuesday, April 7th,

Kick-off 6.15 p.m.

Medals will be presented to the Winning Team by Mr. JAMES SABEL,

The General Manager of the Commodore Theatre, Hammersmith.

| Admission to Ground only | - | 6d. |
| Admission to Enclosure & Stand | | 1/- |

(including Tax).

Children under 14, half-price if they pay at the Gate.

Tickets can be obtained from H. C. Curtis, Griffin Park, Brentford, or any Member of the Branch

COME & HAVE A GOOD LAUGH
AND HELP THE BRITISH LEGION

C. VINCENT EVELEIGH, Hon. Sec., "Cobo," Harvard Road, Gunnersbury

An advertisement for, and photo of, a British Legion comic football match played at Griffin Park in April 1931. The photograph depicts "Sarah Gamp" being chaired!

Fulham's keeper Iceton punches clear.

25th December 1931. Coming into the Christmas and New Year fixture glut of the 1931-32 season, the Bees found themselves sitting pretty three points clear at the top of the Third Division (South) table, and after two near misses, many were quietly confident that this was to be the season for promotion. Having won every league and cup match in December the Bees entertained near neighbours and promotion rivals Fulham on Christmas Day, and, while the game ended goalless, the fixture was a massive crowd-puller, with 26,741 squeezing into Griffin Park:

"While one expected a record crowd, it was not anticipated that the record would be so hopelessly smashed, and hundreds of people turned away. The crowd surged at the turnstiles 6 to 8 deep, and stretched across Braemar Road, making it difficult for the many cars to get by. Four mounted police, aided by many foot police, kept exceedingly good order at Braemar Road. All the surrounding streets were lined with motor cars, and the crowd became so large that the gates had to be closed before the game commenced.

The match had not been in progress very long before the referee, Mr. F.W. Reeve, had to stop it through an alarming scene on the popular side, under the newly erected stand. The crowd had packed itself so tight that the iron railings gave way under pressure and several people had their knees badly bruised as they broke through the barriers on to the pitch. Four policemen crossed the ground to keep the crowd back, and employees of the club roped off the spectators."

(County of Middlesex Independent,
2nd January 1932)

9th January 1932. As the Bees went into their Third Round FA Cup tie against Bath City, football fever had hit west London in a big way. Following the Fulham fixture at Griffin Park, 25,000 had watched the return leg at Craven Cottage, while the 33,508 that saw the Bees triumph 2-1 over QPR at White City made up the highest attendance of any Football League match that day. Amid all this league excitement, the Bees still managed to steady their heads to easily beat Bath 2-0.

Above: Bath's keeper Prout snatches the ball away as Jackie Burns, the Bees' amateur England international wing-half (and schoolteacher), rushes in.

Left: Aerial ballet as both teams vie for the ball.

23rd January 1932.
The Bees had drawn First Division Manchester City out of the hat in the Fourth Round of the FA Cup, and with talk of a repetition of the Cup run enjoyed by the 1926/27 team, a number of supporters decided to make what might very well have been their first trip north on a 'football special' from London;

"Although somewhat gloomy around the district that morning, the spirit of the Cup-tie was lent to the place by the men selling exceptionally good club favours at the station entrance, and the arrival of many supporters with their rattles and bells. Flashlight photographs of the directors and supporters were taken, adding considerably to the fun and merriment. There was plenty of room for everybody on the train, the seats being exceptionally comfortable.

"[The train] stopped...for the first stop, Willesden, to pick up about 300 more supporters, bringing the total to about 800. The journey was very pleasant, not a spot of rain being encountered. White fog clung to the coun-

tryside along parts of the line, but the weather improved as the four hours' journey proceeded.

"The sun came out after Salford had been passed, and when Langsight was reached it was another pleasant surprise to find that the sun continued to shine...The supporters poured out of the train and soon made themselves heard with their rattles, bells and specially (if inartistically) composed songs.

"Manchester City's ground is a mile from the station and two miles from the City. Trams of ancient origin, packed with people, rumbled their way over cobble-stoned roads, and there was no doubt that the natives of Manchester intended being well represented at the match."

(County of Middlesex Independent, 30th January 1932)

Indeed, a crowd of 56,190, the highest to watch a Brentford match up to that date, turned out at Maine Road to enjoy the fixture, and the British Pathe cameras were present to record the competition for posterity. However, the Bees were obviously overawed by the occasion, scoring only once in reply to City's six!

Two stills from the newsreels...

Left: Adamson, Foster, Lane and Nash (r-l) lead out the Bees.

Above: Action from the game with the massive crowd filling the Kippax stand in the background.

30th January 1932.
Following the Bees' Cup
exit at the hands of
Manchester City, their
league form took a turn for
the worse, especially at
home where they lost their
formidable record with a
string of draws. This run
continued against bottom
dogs Gillingham, with Bill
Lane missing a penalty.

*Right: Buckle, the Gills' keeper,
leaps to catch a Brentford
corner kick.*

25th March 1932. The match against Southend United was Brentford's first in a series of eight matches without a win which signalled the end of their promotion hopes. Despite the disappointment on the terraces, however, Second Division football at Griffin Park was soon to be a reality.

Above: Arthur Crompton scores his first goal for the Bees against the side which he had just moved from two weeks previously.

September 3rd 1932. The Bees started the 1932/33 season which would end in promotion in formidable form, winning twelve and drawing two of their first fourteen matches. Here, Torquay United were put to the sword 3-1, with Foster, together with new signings Billy Scott and Jack Holliday, all on the goal sheet.

Below: The referee eyes the penalty area melee from behind a goalpost.

18th March 1933. The 14,000 fans at Griffin Park were shocked as visitors Gillingham inflicted one of only two home defeats that Brentford suffered all season, the other coming at the hands of Exeter City, who pushed the Bees to the wire and eventually finished runners-up.

Above: Bees' centre-half Jimmy Bain (centre) looks on at the goalmouth action.

August 10th 1932. Brentford met Arsenal in a cricket match on the Boston Park Cricket Club ground. For the record, the Bees scored 178 for 9 and won by 13 runs. Bert Watson top-scored with 48 runs.

Below: Jackie Foster attempts a defensive stroke while Arsenal's Baker keeps wicket.

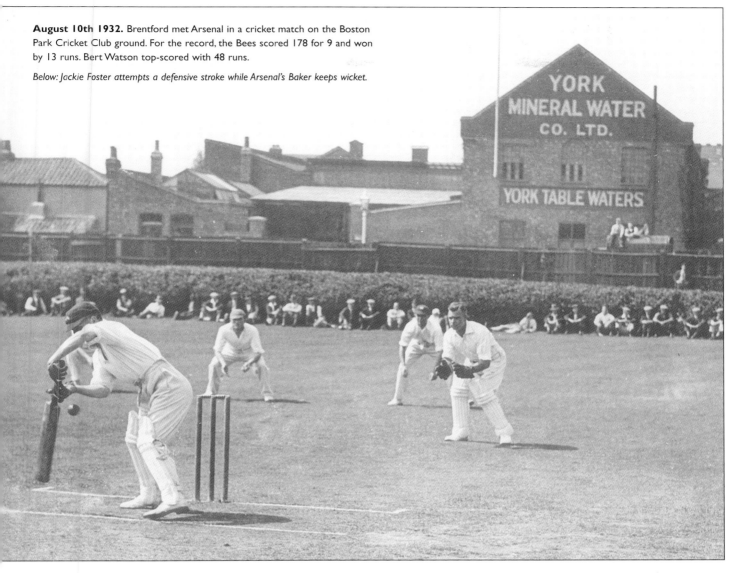

1st April 1933.
Stunned by unexpected defeats against Gillingham and Crystal Palace, and a draw against a mediocre Watford side, Brentford had slipped to third place behind Exeter City and Norwich City, but unlike the near misses of the previous three seasons, the 1932/33 Bees were made of stronger stuff. Roared on by 20,000 vociferous fans, the Bees stuffed a hapless Cardiff City 7-3, Jack Holliday scoring four on his way to a club record 39 goals in 34 league and cup games.

Left: The Cardiff keeper looks on despairingly as Brentford notch another goal.

Photo by] "COME ON THE BEES!" [SIMON
Enthusiastic spectators during another exciting stage in the Brentford and Norwich game.

Left: Jimmy Bain leading out the Brentford team, followed by Hopkins, Muttit, Baker and Lawson, during the Third Division championship season.

15th April 1933. Following the Cardiff City match, the Bees kept up their good work away from home with victories at Reading and Bristol City (playing the latter with only nine men as Jack Holliday and Arthur Crompton were stretchered off), before returning to Griffin Park for the crunch match with promotion rivals Norwich City which ended in a thrilling 2-2 tie.

Above: A section of the 22,000 spectators, the best gate of the season.
Below: Norwich keep a defender on the goal-line as their keeper is squashed in a Brentford attack.

17th April 1933. Two days later, the Bees rounded off a highly satisfactory Easter holiday programme, beating mid-table Bristol City 2-1 with goals from Dai Hopkins and Billy Scott.

Right: Goalkeeper Somerville of Bristol City punches clear from Brentford's Ralph Allen.

Below: Somerville to the rescue again as Hopkins gets stuck in.

Bottom right: Brentford's chairman Louis P. Simon presents the Third Division Championship shield to the team, while the crowd applauds from the pitch.

Brentford's New Covered Terrace

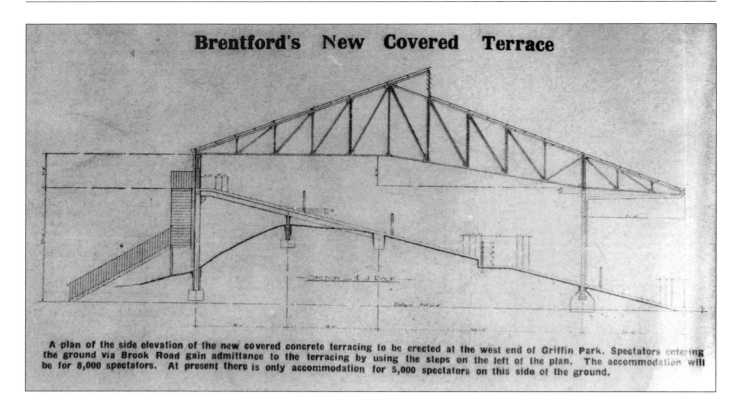

A plan of the side elevation of the new covered concrete terracing to be erected at the west end of Griffin Park. Spectators entering the ground via Brook Road gain admittance to the terracing by using the steps on the left of the plan. The accommodation will be for 8,000 spectators. At present there is only accommodation for 5,000 spectators on this side of the ground.

The summer of 1933 at Griffin Park was spent on the construction of a new covered terrace at the Brook Road end of the ground, with a roof of nearly 100 feet span from front to rear, and capable of accommodating 8,000 spectators. The plans for the stand were outlined in the local press, together with the following justification for the project:

> *"The management realises that the weather, although having little affect on the real football fan where support is concerned, is objected to by many others when the weather is inclined to be wet, and to meet their wishes to view the games in comfort they [Brentford F.C.] have decided upon this ambitious scheme. The Griffin Park ground will now be noted for the fact that it has more covered accommodation than the majority of other clubs.*
> *"The cost of the scheme runs into some thousands of pounds, and will, of course, provide many weeks' work for a large number of men."*

The stand was ready for the Bees' fixture against West Ham United on September 2nd, before which the 25,000 present had enjoyed the raising of a Third Division South Championship flag proudly hoisted behind the goal at the new Brook Road end. The result fitted the occasion as 'Olly Olly' Holliday and Dai Hopkins rattled in two apiece to send the Hammers back east with their tails between their legs.

Top: Plans for the new Brook Road stand.
Left and above: The unfurling of the flag and the new stand before the match.

16th September 1933. The Bees' tremendously confident start to the season took a serious dent as the team let in ten goals in the following three games, including four against bottom of the table Manchester United in a 3-4 home reverse.

Above: Two snaps of Scott (left) and Holliday worrying the United goalkeeper.

9th December 1933. After a lapse of six years Millwall visited Griffin Park, and Scott (twice) and Holliday both delivered as 22,000 Brentford fans delighted in the 3-0 beating of their cross-town neighbours.

Left: Holliday outclimbs everyone to head the ball goalwards, showing off his legendary heading prowess which brought him the vast majority of his goals.

March 17th 1934.
Above: Two shots of Brentford's 1-0 defeat of Blackpool, the winning goal coming from the boot of Dai Hopkins.

Right: An incident from the opening fixture of the promotion-winning 1934/35 season, the Bees defeating Norwich City 2-1 in front of 24,000 fans.

13th January 1935.
Despite coming off the back of a fine 3-0 win over promotion rivals Newcastle United and lying second in the Second Division, Brentford displayed little of the Cup form of their Division Three South days, and for the third season in the row lost their first FA Cup tie, this time against Plymouth Argyle.

Below: Cann, in goal for Plymouth, saves from Scott.

19th April 1935. The Good Friday fixture against Bradford Park Avenue was just that, Brentford holding on to their lead over Bolton Wanderers at the top of the table with a 1-0 win, thereby moving ever closer to the First Division.

Above: Bradford's Farr holds a header from Holliday, the Bees' scorer.

2nd November 1935. The run of bad results through September and October had meant that Brentford had picked up only five points from their last nine matches. But these statistics failed to detract from the enormous levels of excitement and anticipation surrounding the first league visit of the all-conquering League champions, Arsenal, and Brentford confidently expected their biggest ever crowd, feverishly working to further expand Griffin Park in time for the big match. In the event thousands stayed away, scared off by stories of the possibility of catastrophe due to overcrowding, but the 34,000 who were present witnessed a fine 2-0 (Burns, Hopkins) victory for the Bees, thereby establishing a precedent for Bees-Gunners fixtures; during their stay in the top flight, Brentford only lost twice in league competition to Arsenal, once at Griffin Park (1947), and once at Highbury (1939).

Above: Players practice on the pitch as work continues on the Ealing Road terrace (known at the time as the 'bob-a-nob' end) the week before the Arsenal game.
Below: Holliday strikes an acrobatic pose in a tussle with the Arsenal goalkeeper Wilson.

16th November 1935. The Arsenal result proved to be no more than a blip in an otherwise bleak pre-Christmas series of results, the worst coming at the hands of a rampant Sunderland, who netted five to Brentford's one at Griffin Park.

Above: A heading duel in front of the Sunderland goalmouth.

Below: Jack Holliday smiles with band leader Harry Roy and his wife Princess Pearl. The occasion, judging by the plaque on the wall, was the donation of a new bed by Brentford FC at the local hospital.

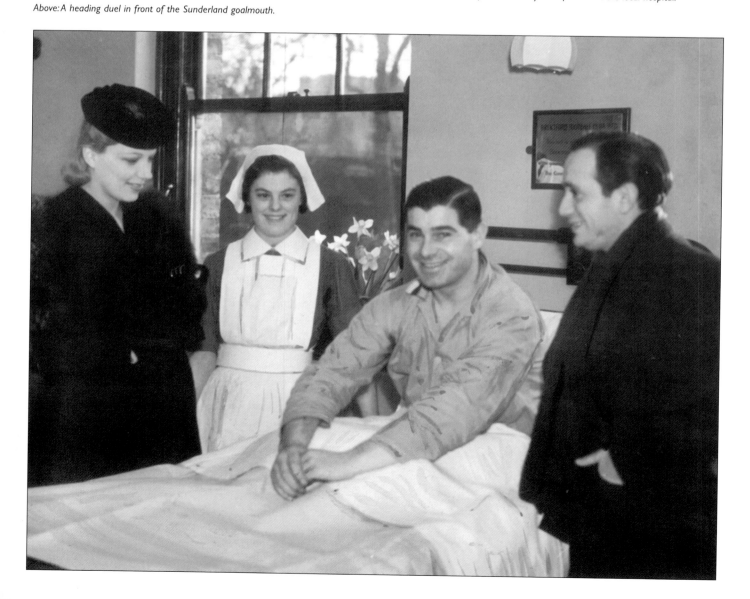

13th October 1936. Impressed by his performance during Brentford's 4-0 trouncing of Manchester United three days earlier, the F.A. Selection Committee had picked Billy Scott to play for England in the international against Wales at Ninian Park the following Saturday. Three Bees were picked for this match; Scott was marked by Dave Richards, and Dai Hopkins also played for Wales.

Right: Scott (being congratulated by manager Harry Curtis), Hopkins and Arthur Bateman.

25th December 1936. Brentford met Sheffield Wednesday on a bright Christmas morning, continuing their excellent home form with a 2-1 win.

Below: Jack Holliday attempts to get his head to the ball and shows off his fine double chin. Bobby Reid, ready to pounce, keeps his eyes fixed on the cross.

2nd January 1937. The Bees concluded a very satisfactory holiday period with a 2-2 draw against Everton at Griffin Park, Brentford's goals coming from Hopkins and a McKenzie penalty.

Far right: Holliday lies on the ground having attempted a diving header.

6th February 1937. Reid, Holliday and McCulloch each grabbed a brace as Brentford hammered Derby County 6-2 at home, avenging their cup exit at the hands of the same team seven days earlier.

Left: Scott just fails to make contact with a Reid centre.

20th March 1937. New signing Bill 'Buster' Brown made his debut in Brentford's easy 4-1 win over Middlesbrough, during which Dave McCulloch scored his second hat-trick of the season, the first coming at home to Liverpool back in October.

Below: Cummings saves at the feet of McCulloch.

29th March 1937.
Right: 35,000 look on as Scott jumps for the ball with McKenzie watching for a rebound during the Good Friday 1-1 draw with Preston North End.

Above: An extremely dapper Brentford squad smile for the camera during their tour of Germany in the summer of 1937.

5th June 1937.
Right: A big day for Dai Hopkins as the Bees' Welsh winger weds his sweetheart Nancy Lane.

August 1937.

Left: Harry Curtis continued the club's spending spree, strengthening the squad with the close season signing of six players: (l to r) coach Bob Kane, Magness 'Jim' Mowatt, George Eastham, Bert Aicken, Harry Curtis, Len Townsend, Joe Crozier, and Bill Sneddon.

August 1937.

Above: (l-r) Dumbrell, Poyser, Wilson, McKenzie, Holliday, McCulloch, Murray and James training for the forthcoming season wearing track suits, which were thought to "greatly help the heavy men in getting their weight down."

Below: Press up training for the players. (l-r) George Dumbrell, Duncan McKenzie, George Poyser, Jack Holliday, Joe Murray, Dave McCulloch, Joe James, Ernie Muttitt, Bill Sneddon.

28th August 1937. Brentford's new inside forward George Eastham had a less than happy start to the season as the Bees went down 2-0 at his old club Bolton Wanderers.

Above: Joe James locks horns with a Bolton striker as Mathieson punches clear.

18th September 1937. *McCulloch powers in one of his two goals which secured a 2-1 defeat of Wolves.*

4th September 1937. Desperate to put in a bid for the championship, Brentford pulled their socks up after the opening day defeat at Burnden Park, winning their next two games against Preston North End and Huddersfield Town.

Two Huddersfield defenders bar Scott's road to goal after a cross from Reid.

Brentford confirmed their position as strong challengers, with eight wins from eleven fixtures between late September and the start of December leaving the Bees at the top of the table.

Right: McCulloch receiving a pass from which he scored one of his two goals during what was by all accounts a truly magnificent Brentford performance against Sunderland on the 2nd of October. The final score was 4-0.

Below: Billy Scott appears to be indulging in a spot of mid-match push-up training as he is felled by the Sunderland goalkeeper.

Bottom: Charlton Athletic's Bartram gets to the ball before Dai Hopkins during Brentford's 5-2 win on the 16th of October.

Leslie Smith puts George Eastham through his paces during training.

23rd October 1937. 56,000 packed Stamford Bridge to watch the west London derby. Leslie Smith's eighteenth minute goal, his first of the season, was not enough for the Bees, Chelsea finishing the game 2-1 winners.

Above: Jack Holliday (on the ground) and Dave McCulloch worry the Chelsea defenders Barber and O'Hare.

8th January 1938. The Bees embarked on one of their finest ever FA Cup runs by dazzling local rivals Fulham and coming away with a resounding 3-1 victory.

Right: Dave McCulloch, scoring one of his two goals, makes doubly sure.

YES, DAVE, IT IS IN ALL RIGHT!

Dave McCulloch, Brentford's centre forward, scoring one of his two goals against

Brentford 'immortals' from the First Division days...

Dai Richards

Dave McCulloch

Leslie Smith

Jack Holliday

Joe James

Dai Hopkins

Billy Scott

Harry Curtis

The 1937/38 season was undoubtedly the finest in Brentford's history, leading the First Division for sixteen consecutive weeks and reaching the last eight of the FA Cup. At the turn of the year, the Bees found themselves as joint favourites to win the championship, and outright favourites to lift the Cup. The exploits of the team, which had been playing in the Third Division a mere five years previously, had swelled local pride and passions to levels which would hardly be imaginable today. Expectations had grown in accordance, and having disposed of Second Division Fulham by three goals to one in the third round of the Cup, the local paper published on the day of the 4th round tie against Portsmouth was hopeful of great things:

"Whatever you think about it, there is no doubt that Brentford is staging at the present time a great bid for the elusive 'double' - League supremacy and the English Cup. A lead of 4 points in Division One at this time of the season is pretty hot stuff, and if Pompey goes down to the locals this afternoon and Monday's draw is kind to them, there you are, my boys..."

Under scrutiny by the media, the Bees' activities in the week prior to the big match were described in great detail:

"The Brentford cup team has spent an enjoyable training week at its old headquarters, the Bushey Hall Hotel. Light ball practice, golf, country walks, swimming and indoor games kept them fit and fresh.

"The team was encouraged to keep its mind off today's game. On Tuesday the players saw the show at the Chiswick Empire, and on Wednesday they visited the London Palladium. Thursday night saw them at an ice hockey match at Wembley, and on Friday afternoon a visit was paid to Bertram Mills' Circus at Olympia. At this circus Dave McCulloch took a penalty kick in the wonderfully staged football game between teams of

Happy fans at the match.

elephants! The elephants were got up in the Bees' colours. The big crowd yelled as Dave hit the ball. The rest of Friday was spent quietly, and after an early night the team will come up to Brentford today by motor coach."

(County of Middlesex Independent, 22nd January 1938)

On the day of the match itself, thousands swarmed into Griffin Park to watch the contest. As the terraces filled up...

"there were amazing scenes just before kick-off. Hundreds of small boys jumped over the railings, and the crowd threw down to them clouds of papers to sit on as the ground was damp. The situation developed into too much of a good thing, and a loud-speaker appeal was made to the crowd to cease throwing them down because they were littering up the playing area."

By all accounts the game itself was a spectacle fit to match the occasion. The correspondent for the County of Middlesex Independent of 29th January certainly enjoyed it...

"What a game! This is the most thrilling game I have ever witnessed - a full 90 minutes of red-blooded football, with fierce tackling and lightning exchanges forming a sensation-packed background for some of the cleverest top speed football I have ever seen. Those two teams battling out there before a record crowd of 37,000 gave us all they had in the way of courage, endurance and sheer, unadulterated guts.

"Pompey lost. But its gallant battle will be remembered at Griffin Park until there is no longer a Griffin Park or a Brentford Football Club. Portsmouth played brilliantly in the first half, its slick accuracy in mid-field had Brentford worried. Let there be no mistake about it, the visitors took all the glory in the first 45 minutes. The second half held out a different story. It is true that Brentford eventually equalised through a penalty kick, but I think it would have equalised anyway. No longer did Brentford keep the ball in the air, forcing McCulloch and the wingers to face their own goal in an endeavour to collect the passes aimed at them. Scott and Holliday, Brown and Sneddon carried the ball up to them and broke up anything in the way of a constructive move with even more efficiency than Pompey had done in the first half."

"Brentford discovered its snap and accuracy in ball distribution, and going ahead through Dave McCulloch - and what a goal he got! - held its mastery until the end."

Left: Young supporters congregate by the touchline at the Ealing Road end.

Above: The Brentford defence clear their lines.
Below: Joe Crozier leaps to smother the danger of a Pompey corner.

12th February 1938. Brentford disposed of Second Division frontrunners Manchester United 2-0 in the 5th round of the FA Cup, one goal coming from Holliday in the first half, the other from Bobby Reid two minutes before the final whistle.

Right: A cross comes into the goalmouth where Scott tries a header as Breen punches clear. Brentford played in their away strip of white shirts with black shorts, even though the game was held at Griffin Park.

Below: Head tennis with (l-r) Billy Scott, Ernie Muttit, Len Townsend, Leslie Smith and Joe James.

Right: Brentford's skipper Arthur Bateman shakes hands with boxer Tommy Farr before a match in 1938, much to the delight of the other players and fans. Tommy had won the British and Empire heavyweight title the previous year, and had gone on to lose to Joe Louis on a disputed points decision in what was arguably one of the most courageous heavyweight title challenges ever.

February 1938. The players had begun to focus increasingly on their approaching tie with Preston North End in the 6th round of the Cup, and consecutive defeats against Sunderland, Derby County and Charlton Athletic meant both Arsenal and Wolverhampton Wanderers overtaking the Bees at the top of the table.

Jack Holliday challenges the Derby keeper Kirby as McCulloch runs in to help.

Dave McCulloch is denied a goal scoring opportunity by Valiants' keeper Sam Bartram.

Brentford's full-back Bill Brown competes for the ball with Charlton's centre-forward Owens during the match at the Valley, watched by 45,000 fans.

1940s

30th May 1942. With the armed forces embroiled in battle with Germany, Brentford F.C. were busying themselves entertaining the populace of west Middlesex, and providing some relief from the dark business of war. Before the regionalisation of the Football League prior to the start of the 1941/42 season, travel costs were proving to be an appalling drain on the resources of many clubs already struggling to field a side every week, and Brentford had contemplated closing down for the duration of the conflict. In retrospect, it was just as well that the Bees opted to remain open for competitive football, as the season was to culminate with a Wembley victory in front of the biggest congregation of people ever to see the team perform. Having achieved top spot in their qualifying group of the London War Cup, which included Millwall, QPR and Aldershot, the Bees braved Arsenal in the semi-final at Stamford Bridge. Watched by 41,154, the game finished a goalless draw, so a replay date was set for a fortnight later at White Hart Lane (which, at the time, was Arsenal's home ground). Another gate in excess of 40,000 saw Brentford overcome the Gunners by two goals to one, setting up a date with Portsmouth at Wembley to challenge for the Cup.

Although obviously not the "real thing", i.e. an FA Cup Final, the interest that the event aroused surprised many, and with a restricted capacity in force tickets were at a premium. In fact, newspapers of the day reported on the trouble caused by the wholesale purchase of higher priced tickets by touts who attempted to sell them on at inflated prices outside the ground. (Some things never change!)

Still, those Brentford fans among the 71,500 present looking for a good omen must have been cheered by the sight of the goals; they were Brentford's, dismantled at Griffin Park the previous week and re-assembled at Wembley! And so it proved to be, as the Bees overturned the pre-match favourites by a 2-0 scoreline, both goals coming from the dazzling Leslie Smith. In fact, Leslie's second goal was, by all accounts, one of the finest yet seen at Wembley. Not that his preparation for the contest was ideal, as he later recounted...

"My £28 car broke down and left me stranded miles from Wembley Stadium, where in fifty minutes I was due to take part in the South Cup Final. We were half way up a steep hill, and from experience I knew the only way to get the car started would be to reach the top and let her run down. In my eagerness to reach Wembley I tried to get a lift from passing motorists. As they all went by I became more and more agitated.

"After much vain effort to persuade the engine to tick over, Alf Chalkley, the West Ham back who was one of my passengers, helped in the long push up the hill. Soon afterwards we were travelling towards Wembley at a speed that threatened to make our ancient car fall to pieces.

"Fifteen minutes to go - and bang! - we were in a long line of traffic. Cars, buses and taxis stretched like a long finger in front of us. We took every possible chance to make headway through that crowd. Men waved their fists at us and said we were taking liberties...but on we went.

"With eight minutes to go we reached the Stadium. I jumped out, grabbed my bag and left it to Alf to put the car away. "Where have you been?" was the welcome I received. "We thought you must have been hurt. You'll have to hurry." That was an understatement. The twelfth man was slipping off his coat when I dashed into the dressing room.

"My switching from RAF uniform into Brentford shirt must have beaten anything achieved even by a demobbed man changing into 'civvies'. Within five minutes I was on the field and had scored the first goal! Two minutes from the end I scored again and Brentford had won the Cup."

Above: Fred Durrant (right) relaxes at his digs in Hounslow with keeper Saunders (left) and C. Brown, who played four times for the Bees during the 1944/45 season.

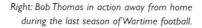

Right: Bob Thomas in action away from home during the last season of Wartime football.

12th April 1947. The Bees' inability to score on a regular basis during the first post-War season ultimately cost the club their position in the top division as the team gained both points on only one occasion following their improbable win over Wolves on January 18th. Brentford's lack of fire-power was highlighted once again with a 0-0 draw at home to Manchester United.

Below: United's right back Johnny Carey, who had played for both Eire and Northern Ireland like the Bees' Bill Gorman, in a tussle for the ball with Girding.

The 1946/47 squad in relaxed mood while visiting a film set.

23rd August 1947.
Brentford travelled to Craven Cottage, Fulham, for their first fixture back in the Second Division. A number of pre-War favourites, such as Hopkins, Brown, Muttit, Boulter and Scott had been given free transfers, and the supporters' scepticism about the squad's lack of league experience was confirmed as Fulham scored five without reply.

Right: The teams take to the field led by captains Tom Manley for Brentford and Fulham's Joe Bacuzzi.
Below: Joe Crozier in action.

20th September 1947.
Right: Frank Hodgetts (extreme right) is foiled by Joe Crozier at The Hawthorns as the Bees went down 3-2 to West Bromwich Albion in this Second Division clash.

24th January 1948.

The win over Rotherham United in the third round of the FA Cup, compounded by a heartening 1-0 victory against promotion challengers Newcastle United, had lifted spirits after the nightmare year of 1947 which had seen Brentford fall from the First Division to the relegation zone of the Second, and 34,500 converged on Griffin Park to watch the Cup match against Middlesbrough.

Referee G. Tedds, however, appeared unhappy with this mini-revival; with time fast running out, Jackie Gibbons was felled in Middlesbrough's box, but instead of awarding the blatantly obvious penalty decision in the home team's favour, he allowing Boro to break and score the winner while the Brentford players stood aghast, arguing the decision.

A A large queue forms outside the Braemar Road stand and continues past the Princess Royal Public House into Ealing Road.

B Brentford's captain Malcolm MacDonald leads the team out, followed by Joe Crozier.

C All eyes on the coin just before kick-off.

D Dickie Girling gives Brentford the lead.

E Celebrations at the Ealing Road end, especially from the kid at the front!

F (l-r) Dave Nelson, Joe Crozier and Malcolm MacDonald defend their goal.

G Surrounded by Boro players, Tommy Dawson scraps for the ball.

H John Spuhler equalises for Middlesbrough in the second half.

20th April 1948.
Above: Malcolm MacDonald, who played in all but one fixture during the 1947/48 season at the heart of the Bees' defence, climbs high during the match at Southampton.

21st August 1948. The first game of the 1948/49 season, which was to be the last with manager Harry Curtis at the helm, saw the Bees share four goals with Coventry City, a gate of 26,031 enjoying the 2-2 draw.

Above: The Bees' centre-half Jack Chisholm heads out from a Coventry attack.

March 1950.

Out of the blue Brentford F.C. had received a "very signal honour", being invited by the Netherlands Football Association to play the full Dutch international team as a warm up for their forthcoming match against Belgium. Needless to say the offer was gratefully accepted, and the team travelled to Holland for the match, as recalled by manager Jackie Gibbons:

"On Monday 27th March, a party of twenty took off from London Airport for Amsterdam, Holland, arriving there one hour and twenty-five minutes later. The flight itself was perfect and for those half-dozen of our party who had never flown before, they enjoyed a very pleasant initiation. In the evening we visited the cinema and on the following morning, much to the surprise of some of the Netherlands F.A. Officials, the thirteen players, plus Malcolm MacDonald and "yours truly", did nearly two hours' training at the Sparta Stadion. In the afternoon we were taken on a sight-seeing tour through the Amsterdam canals, seeing many points of historical interest.

"We left Amsterdam at 10.30 on Wednesday morning and stopped for lunch at a very beautiful castle at "Old Wassenaar". We later left for Rotterdam, passing through the Hague, and arriving at the Feijnoord Stadion in good time for the game.

"Approximately 63,000 people [the second largest congregation ever to watch the Bees] had come to see the match, and a great deal of importance had been paid to the game in the press. Our own lads also realised the importance of the game, both from a national and club aspect. Tom Manley won the toss and the Dutch team kicked off and went straight to the attack. Fortunes fluctuated throughout the first half, which was played with great speed; the Dutch midfield play and approach work

was first class, but they met a resolute Bees' defence determined not to give the Dutch boys the slightest shooting chance.

"Half-time arrived with a clear score-sheet, and on the resumption it was clear for all to see that the Dutch team were intent on finding our net; this they did do once, but the referee had previously whistled, the ball having passed over the bye-line and been brought back into play. Shortly afterwards, Billy Pointon netted for the Bees, but the goal was disallowed, quite rightly, for offside. The game had not slackened in pace, and both teams were attacking and defending and doing their utmost to notch a goal. The final whistle arrived, however, with a blank score sheet, a fitting result to a grand game full of good football, played in the finest sporting spirit by both teams.

"The party returned to Amsterdam by coach after the match, and were entertained at a banquet in the hotel by members of the Netherlands F.A., whose Vice-President paid many high compliments to the Bees and presented a silver bowl to the club, a plaque bearing the Netherlands F.A. badge, and a unique pair of cuff links to every member of our party. The team remained over until mid-day Friday, when the K.L.M. 'plane brought us back to London Airport, and the curtain rang down on what had proved to be one of the grandest trips we shall ever be privileged to make."

Above: Fred Monk and Alf Jefferies defend their goal as Lakenberg, on the ground, fails to connect with a cross.

Right: Jefferies saves from Roosenburg. Wally Quinton stands guard on the goal line, while Ron Greenwood (number 6) marks his man.

16th July 1950.

Above: A handshake of welcome for the new season's recruits to Brentford on the first day of light training back at Griffin Park prior to the 1950/51 season. Unlike the old First Division days, money was tight and manager Jackie Gibbons had to rely on the promise of non-league youngsters.

(l-r) vice-captain Ron Greenwood, T. Jones, George Bristow (the youngest player on Brentford's books and one who was of course to stay at the club for over a decade), future England international Peter Broadbent, R. Hart, and captain Tom Manley.

Right: Frank Latimer jumps highest during a pre-season training match between probables and possibles.

26th August 1950.
Brentford's first home game of the 1950/51 season against Leeds United attracted 20,381 fans, who saw the Yorkshiremen run out 2-1 winners.

Left: Jeffries makes a high save from Harrison, the Leeds' outside right, while Roddie Munro runs back to cover.

13th January 1951.

Left: Alf Jefferies, protected by Tony Harper, picks off the ball during Brentford's 1-2 reverse at Swansea Town.

7th April 1951.
The two last-gasp goals from Jackie Goodwin (left) and Billy Dare (above) that gave Brentford both points at Leicester City.

18th August 1951. The new campaign, starting with a tricky away fixture at Leeds United's Elland Road, commenced on a promising note, Brentford coming back from an early deficit to gain a 1-1 draw through a goal from John Paton.

Top left: Jefferies and Greenwood close in on United's centre-forward Browning.

6th October 1951. Ken Coote notched a late winner to give Brentford a 1-0 success over Notts County, the crowd of 29,500 showing the renewed faith of the Middlesex fans in the ability of the Bees, with their fine defensive record, to more than just survive in the Second Division.

Below: John Paton roars in from the left wing as the Magpies' keeper Smith clears.
Left: Paton again, this time in a tussle for the ball with Notts centre half Leuty.

12th January 1952. Amid the rancour surrounding the sudden transfer listing of the fans' favourites Jimmy Hill and Ron Greenwood due to dressing room discord, the new year saw the Bees being drawn out of the hat against local rivals QPR in the 3rd round of the FA Cup. An all-ticket crowd of 35,000 packed Griffin Park, with the Bees winning 3-1 through goals by Coote, Paton and Sperrin, setting up a classic three match marathon with Luton Town in the 4th round.

Above: Brentford's left back Ken Horne in a heading duel with QPR's Shepherd.

6th February 1952. Having drawn 2-2 at Luton Town in the 4th round, the replay at Griffin Park again produced a stalemate as both sides failed to score after extra time.

Below: Ron Greenwood and Jimmy Hill (wearing number 6) are heavily marked by at least nine Luton players.

18th February 1952. The Bees met the Hatters for the second cup replay at Arsenal's Highbury. 37,269 saw Brentford twice equalise through Billy Dare, before finally surrendering with Luton's third of the afternoon.

Right: Ted Gaskell, in goal for the injured Jeffries, holds the ball to his chest while Ron Greenwood and Ken Horne look on.

1st March 1952. Brentford again met Luton Town, in the league this time, and shared a further six goals in an end-to-end tussle.

Below: Billy Dare (not in picture) scores Brentford's second goal, as Ken Horne, playing his one and only game at centre-forward, gets stuck in. Luton's Ahearne and keeper Stretton can't believe it.
Facing page: A fine picture of determination from Ken Horne.

14th March 1952. Brentford pulled off the shock signing of the year, gaining the services of Tommy Lawton from Notts County for £16,000. Although he was not the force he had been during his earlier days at Everton and Chelsea, Tommy was still regarded as something of a football immortal, and, it was felt, would bring immeasurable skill, generalship and shooting power to Griffin Park.

Above: Brentford's vice-chairman Mr. H. Davis pats the shoulder of his new signing as Lawton reads over his contract with Jackie Gibbons. British Pathe newsreels recorded the occasion, Tommy smiling "Well Jack, I'm very glad to be back in London, and I'm very pleased to be coming to Brentford."

15th March 1952. The arrival of Tommy Lawton had seized the interest of the local populace; despite a run of nine league and cup matches without a win, 31,000 clicked through the Griffin Park turnstiles to watch the great man play in the red, white and black for the first time, cheering every time he touched the ball. Tommy's presence, together with the resultant atmosphere, had the desired effect as the Bees beat Swansea Town by three goals to one.

Above: Lawton, wearing the number 9 shirt, feels the weight of a tackle from Town's centre-half Weston.

Left: The ball hits the back of the net for the Bees' first goal, set up by a headed pass from Lawton and scored by Ken Coote, lying on the ground.

Right: Man-of-the-moment Lawton is robbed of the ball by Swansea's keeper Johnny King.

Despite relegation, pre-season optimism abounded, and this confidence was heightened through the season by a number of impressive big money signings such as Billy McAdams from Leeds United, West Ham's John Dick, and Mel Scott from Chelsea. From early on, Brentford, together with Oldham Athletic, set the pace, and by the run in to the end of the season the match between the two at Boundary Park was being billed as a clash of the titans. 17,771 watched the Latics gain a fortuitous 2-1 victory, a Billy McAdams header disallowed literally on the stroke of ninety minutes, but three wins and a draw in their final five fixtures was enough to give the Bees the Championship and promotion at the first time of asking.

Top: Fred Rycraft dives at the feet of the onrushing Oldham forward, with Peter Gelson in attendance.

Centre: A Latics striker slips the ball under Rycraft. Ken Coote looks on from the wing.

Bottom: Tom Anthony darts in for the challenge.

May 23rd 1963. *Above: A line of local bobbies struggle to hold back a mob of ecstatic supporters celebrating Brentford's promotion on the pitch after the Bees' 4-3 win over Workington on the last day of the season.*

Below: Ken Coote and chairman Jack Dunnett admire the Fourth Division Championship cup.

Right: Work commences behind the Braemar Road stand, creating the same frontage that is still present today.

Below: The new floodlights at Griffin Park are given a 'trial run' with a friendly against QPR before the start of the 1963/64 season. 8,000 largely satisfied customers saw Brentford win 4-1.

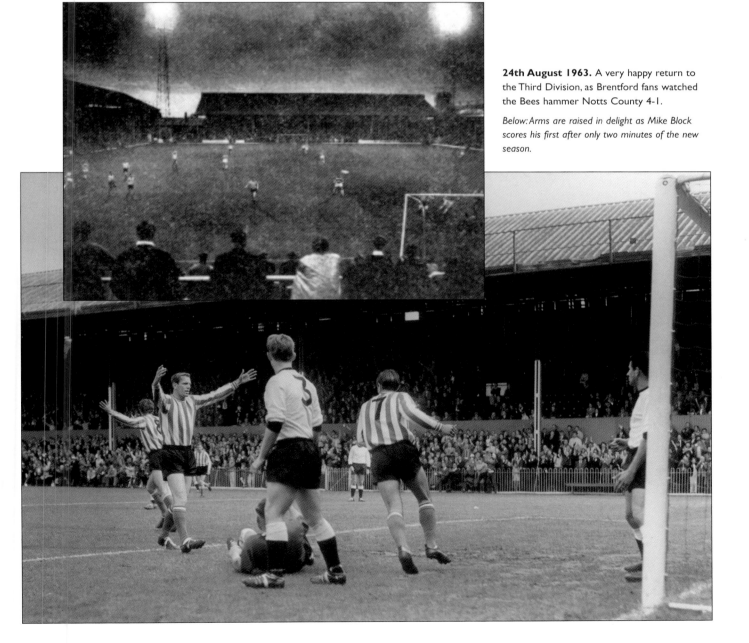

24th August 1963. A very happy return to the Third Division, as Brentford fans watched the Bees hammer Notts County 4-1.

Below: Arms are raised in delight as Mike Block scores his first after only two minutes of the new season.

7th September 1963.
Right: Billy McAdams' header skims the top of the net during the Bees' 2-1 win over Crystal Palace, enjoyed by a bumper attendance of 15,800.

5th October 1963. Brentford played host to promotion favourites and eventual champions Coventry City, and despite goals from Dick and McAdams, went down by the odd goal to the West Midlands side managed by former Bee Jimmy Hill.

Below: Dick and Hales involved in a goalmouth melee during the game against the Sky Blues.

15th October 1963. Suffering from a 2-5 drubbing at home at the hands of Bristol Rovers three days earlier, manager Malcolm MacDonald felt changes were necessary. Gerry Cakebread, Ken Coote, Tommy Higginson, George Summers and Johnny Brooks all returned to the team, which was additionally strengthened by the signing of Watford's Welsh international Dai Ward for £8,000. The changes certainly worked....

"Variety is said to be the spice of life. If so, these are very spicy days for Brentford's followers, for after the third consecutive home defeat...the Bees took the field again on Wednesday to net nine goals against Wrexham. Apart from wartime regional league games, this was the highest score in the club's history, just pipping the previous best total of eight against Barnsley, Port Vale and Bury.

"The gate-lowering effect of Saturday's disappointing exhibition and the threat of evening rain were offset to some extent by the presence of a newly signed player, but the crowd (10,500) was the smallest muster for a league game at Griffin Park this season. But they made enough noise for twice that number as the goals piled up - always with the promise of another one in the immediate future - and if there had been a roof to Griffin Park at the start, it would have been lifted off before the finish. As it was, the rousing ovation accorded to the Bees at the interval was encored as they trooped off for the bath.

"Ward, of course, was the focal point for every eye, and no on-looker could have been dissatisfied with what he saw. He was a non-stop forager and schemer, and in addition to getting two goals for himself, he had a foot in the build-up of four others. But Ward wasn't the only star on view. Ten other players made their individual and collective contributions to the record victory."

"The remarkable feature about the match was that four of the five goals in the opening half came from corners.

"It was 1-0 after three minutes as McAdams met the ball just beyond the far post to volley past Fleet, and the Bees scored again after another three minutes, Ward scoring with a deft overhead kick from Hales' corner.

"With quarter of an hour gone, Fleet was beaten for a third time. Hales took the flag-kick. Brooks shot, and the ball turned into the net off McAdams as he squatted on the ground.

"The Wrexham centre-half, Fox, sent the ball between the legs of his own keeper and into the empty net for the fourth home goal, and the fifth came when Hales nodded in a right-wing corner by Brooks.

"In the second half, there was no let-up in the goal storm. Brooks, taking a pass from Ward, swivelled to hit the only long-range goal of the night; and when Fleet went down to push out a shot from Ward, the loose-running ball was tapped in

Above: Action from the record victory with Summers, Slater and Coote involved in the play.

Right: A rare attack on the Bees' goal is foiled by Cakebread, who punches clear from Wrexham's inside left Metcalf, flanked by Slater and Coote.

by Summers for number seven.

"The eighth goal was a weirdie. Seized with a sudden spasm of cramp in the act of shooting, Brooks miskicked; but the ball took a curly course, and when everybody thought it would go over the bar, it dipped into the net.

"The only question remaining to be answered was 'would Brentford break the club record?' ...and with only a few seconds of the hour and a half to run, Ward put the finishing touch to a memorable occasion by driving in the ninth goal."

26th October 1963, and 15,200 turned up to see the Bees defeat visitors Millwall by three goals to one.

Above: Eagle eyes from Mike Block watching the touchline action.

16th November 1963. Southern League Margate visited Griffin Park in the First Round of the FA Cup, coming away with a 2-2 draw thanks to a late fumble from a young Gordon Phillips making his debut. The lower division team were not to prove an obstacle, however, Brentford winning the replay 2-0.

Ken Coote runs on to a lofted ball.

Above: (l-r) Mark Lazarus, Billy McAdams, Dai Ward and John Fielding in goalmouth action from 1963/64.

January 4th 1964. Despite their erratic form in the league, the team was still in the FA Cup come the new year having beaten non-league Gravesend & Northfleet in the Second Round, and were drawn at home in the Third Round to Middlesbrough. The prospect of putting one over higher division opposition drew more than 16,000 to Griffin Park, and the fans were not to be disappointed as the Bees ran out 2-1 winners with goals from Dick and McAdams.

Right: Brodie outleaps Scott and Middlesbrough's Peacock to punch clear, while Thomson and Jones guard the Bees' goal.

January 25th 1964.
Victory over the Teesiders set up a Fourth Round tie away to new boys Oxford United, who were enjoying only their second season in the Football League. The 15,157 present at the Manor Ground saw Brentford take the lead twice through Ward and Block, but the home side levelled the score twice to take the match to a replay at Griffin Park. The 4th Division side cancelled out a McAdams strike to win 2-1 in front of a huge crowd of 26,000, and went on to reach the Sixth Round.

Mike Block, obscured by Dai Ward, knocks in Brentford's first at the Manor Ground.

Above: Mel Scott takes a tumble, 1963/64.

22nd August 1964.
Chairman Jack Dunnett had continued to spend in the search for success, signing Jimmy Bloomfield and Joe Bonson for a total of £18,000 in the off-season months, and it was the latter who made his mark in the first game of the 1964/65 season, scoring twice in a 2-2 draw at home to Luton Town on the first day of the new campaign.

Right: (l-r) Bonson, Ward, McAdams and Fielding look on as the Luton 'keeper saves.

5th September 1964.
Right: Joe Bonson in action as Brentford ran riot over Port Vale, finishing the game as 4-0 winners. This win marked the start of a fine series of results which led to the Bees topping the table through much of September and October.

26th November 1964.
Left: Ian Lawther and his wife arrive at the House of Commons with Brentford's manager Malcolm MacDonald to complete the transfer of the Northern Ireland international from Scunthorpe for £17,000. The occasion took place at the invitation of Brentford chairman Jack Dunnett, Labour MP for Nottingham Central.

19th December 1964.
With other new signings Billy Cobb and Mark Lazarus complementing an already strong team, Brentford had developed into an exciting, free-scoring outfit, scoring no less than sixteen goals in the five games prior to the pre-Christmas clash with Carlisle. But the Bees really turned on the style against the future champions, demolishing the northeners 6-1, with Billy Cobb netting what was by all accounts a quite exceptional hat-trick.

Below: Cobb scores his third of the afternoon.

Top right: Lawther beats the stranded Carlisle keeper for Brentford's fourth.

26th December 1964.
One week on, Brentford complemented the Carlisle win with victory over their other promotion rivals Bristol City, 16,065 enjoying the Boxing Day fare.

Right: Billy Cobb leads the attack on the Ealing Road end.

12th January 1965. Amid great excitement surrounding the exploits of the Brentford team, a quite enormous crowd of 30,448, the largest at Griffin Park since Sheffield Wednesday were there on Good Friday morning 1952, turned up on a Tuesday evening to watch the Bees take on First Division Burnley in the Third Round FA Cup replay. Favourable reports of Brentford's gritty display at Turf Moor had whetted local appetites for a giant-killing, but although for seventy minutes of the match Burnley led by no more than a slender one goal margin, the northeners seldom let the game slip away from their grasp.

The Bees' biggest moment of frustration; the ball, from Fielding's header, bounces down from the underside of the bar. Brentford players argued that it had struck the ground goal-side of the line, but the referee ruled otherwise.
Where was the Russian linesman?

16th January 1965. *Right: Ian Lawther strikes the ball wide of the target during the match against lowly Colchester United which the Bees won thanks to a Peter Gelson goal.*

13th February 1965. Intent on staying in the frame for promotion, the club was shocked by the sudden announcement that manager Malcolm MacDonald, who had links with the club dating back to 1946 and who had been in charge since 1957, had given notice and intended to return to Kilmarnock as secretary/manager. Coach Tommy Cavanagh was hastily appointed as acting manager, with future Bees boss Jimmy Sirrel at his side, and the Bees kept up the pressure with an unexpected win at leaders Bristol Rovers. This was followed up by a 2-2 draw at home to Oldham Athletic, Brentford bouncing back from two down to equalise with two second half goals from Lazarus and Lawther. Unfortunately, despite their continued excellent home form, the team failed to capitalise on the situation finishing in fifth place (three points off top spot), and the season could only be summed up as a near miss.

Below: Dai Ward in an acrobatic tangle against Oldham.
Bottom: New Road fans watch Ward and Lawther on the attack.

14th September 1965. The 4-0 victory over Shrewsbury proved to be one of only three or four bright spots in an otherwise desperate season which many expected would see the Bees clinch promotion but which ended, despite a change of manager (Billy Gray replacing the fired Tommy Cavanagh), in relegation.

Bottom right: Billy Cobb gets up well as Bonson looks on.

6th November 1965.
Left: A policeman holds the unexploded hand grenade - with the pin removed - thrown at Brentford's goalkeeper Chic Brodie during the match against Millwall at Griffin Park.

Above: Lawther, Etheridge (in the background) and Regan attacking during the 1966/67 season.

10th January 1967.
Right: John Docherty gets the ball past keeper Ron Willis to give the Bees their second goal in a 3-1 victory over Leyton Orient in the Second Round of the FA Cup. Brentford went on to lose 2-5 away at First Division Sunderland in the next round.

November 1966. *The cameras are let in for one of the regular ballet classes at Griffin Park. Dance teacher Doreen Hermitage, leading the lessons, commented "I feel that my little sessions are helping the boys with their poise and balance, and they've had fewer pulled muscles while playing. But you couldn't print what some of them said when they heard they were to have ballet lessons!" Cue jokes about transfers to Saddlers Wells and dancing the ball into the opponents net.*

With relegation from the Third Division at the end of the 1966/67 season, which itself had started with such high hopes, gates were well down, and the club was losing money hand over fist. With Chairman Jack Dunnett announcing large losses on the last financial year, and arguing that the club was no longer a financially viable concern, the Bees were thrust onto the front pages of the national press on January 19th 1967 as news emerged of a scheme, concocted by Jack Dunnett and QPR's chairman Jim Gregory, to merge the two clubs at the end of the 1966/67 season, a move that would effectively signal the demise of Brentford F.C. Supporters were incensed; over 10,000 fans, way up on the season's average, turned out at Griffin Park for the match against Southend United two days later to voice their anger and frustration, and to show their allegiance and commitment to Brentford Football Club, as recalled by the Middlesex Chronicle of 27th January...

"Even an hour before kick-off time on Saturday, only a moron could have failed to feel that there was much more hanging over Griffin Park than the result of the afternoon's game with Southend. Banners were aloft, television interviews were being conducted with anyone who happened to be near the mike, groups of fans were huddled together in anxious confab over the threatened takeover; and even thus early it was obvious that the attendance would top the figure for any previous home league game this season.

"The Bees, already highly tensed in view of the crisis in the club's affairs, were further infected by the excitement coming over the touchlines. Southend looked the more settled side in the first half, and on 23 minutes, United went ahead. McKinven sent the ball forward, and Flatt shot past Phillips as the keeper raced out. But in the 53rd minute, the crowd almost roared the roof off the stand as Brentford equalised. George Thomson, in his sweeper-up role, collected a stray ball near the centre circle and moved slickly through the middle to send a perfect pass out to Ross on the left wing. The Brentford skipper forced a corner, and that corner did the trick. From the flag, Ross curled a ball over to the far post, and Lawther, bending almost double, headed into the opposite corner, well away from Roberts.

Opposite and above: Supporters signing petitions and displaying banners demonstrating against the proposed takeover.

Above left: The Bees' inside forward Ian Lawther (second right) gets his head to the ball as John South also leaps.

Left: Lawther nods home a powerful header to equalise.

23rd October 1971.
Despite the shock sale of the popular Roger Cross to Fulham which had angered fans desperate for success, Brentford's free-scoring start to the season had the crowds flooding back, and the visit of promotion rivals Southend United drew the best Griffin Park attendance since 1965 (14,001). Unfortunately the visitor's 2-1 victory heralded a poor run of results over November which saw Brentford drop from first to fourth in the table and go out of the FA Cup at the first hurdle.

Above: An injury stoppage allows Peter Gelson and Brian Turner to join the Southend players in taking a break.

27th December 1971.
Back to their winning ways in December, another John O'Mara header allowed Brentford to record their fourth straight win, this time against Crewe Alexandra.

Left: Big John makes his towering presence known. In the background is a packed New Road terrace, containing some of the 18,237 rejuvenated Bees fans.

8th January 1972. Drawing 1-1 at half time against lowly Darlington, Brentford served notice of what they were capable of by notching five times in the second half, the goals being shared between John Docherty and John O'Mara.

Above: The Darlington defence work up a sweat trying to contain Brian Turner and Bobby Ross.

Below: Three of the main reasons for the Bees' successful promotion challenge in 1971/72; John Docherty, John O'Mara and Bobby Ross.

20th April 1974. *Above: Sixteen-year-old Kevin Harding lines up for a shot during Brentford's 2-0 victory over Bradford City. With Brentford finishing in their lowest ever Division Four placing, the points gained in this match enabled Brentford to avoid a humiliating application for re-election, thus drawing a curtain on what was easily one of the Bees' most depressing seasons in their Football League history.*

10th September 1974. Having disposed of Aldershot in the First Round of the Football League Cup, Brentford travelled to face First Division giants Liverpool in the next round. The 21,413 present at Anfield held their breath in anticipation of a cup upset as the Bees, playing in their yellow second strip, scored an early goal through Roger Cross and kept their lead for twenty minutes, before Ray Kennedy and Phil Boersma scored one apiece to give the Reds the victory.

Below: Peter Gelson, Keith Lawrence, Micky Allen and Steve Sherwood fail to stop a Liverpool goal.
Inset: Beaten but happy - Dave Metchik and Steve Sherwood commiserate over tea and lemonade after the game.

Brentford started the 1975/76 season in reasonable form, winning three and drawing three of their first six matches, including this 1-1 result at home to Hartlepool United.

b) *Dave Simmons (number 9) eyes the ball as Terry Johnson takes a shot on goal which was saved by keeper Richardson.*

22nd November 1975.
c) *Gordon Sweetzer in full steam, on the way to scoring the first of two goals which put Bill Dodgin's high-flying Northampton Town out of the FA Cup.*

13th December 1975.
With their defeat of Northampton Town, a Terry Johnson brace at Southern League Wimbledon's Plough Lane gave Brentford a reasonably untroubled 2-0 win in the Second Round.

d) *Terry rounds the keeper to fire home his first of the match.*

6th January 1976. Having reached the Third Round of the FA Cup for the first time since their celebrated 1970/71 run, Brentford were drawn against First Division Bolton Wanderers.

22nd March 1975.
a) *Jackie Graham fights for possession during Brentford's 1-1 draw with Chester City. This fixture came in the middle of a much improved series of results as Mike Everitt's successor John Docherty (back at Griffin Park for the fourth time) pulled the Bees away from the re-election zone in January to an end-of-season eighth place spot.*

23rd August 1975.
Skippered by Paul Bence,

12,450 saw the Bees manage a 0-0 draw at home, before succumbing to the superior class of the Lancastrians in the replay.

e) *Neil Whatmore, scorer of both Bolton's goals, fires a low shot towards Paul Priddy in goal for the Bees at Burnden Park.*

16th April 1976.
f) *Swansea City keeper Steve Potter runs out to stop an attack spearheaded by Roger Cross and, in the background, new signing and future favourite Andy McCulloch. The match finished 1-0, Brentford recording one of only five wins achieved in the new year, a*

series of results which left the Bees placed 18th by the end of the season.

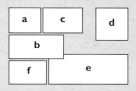

Top left: Mike French wows the babes with his trendy new sweater; the height of fashion exclusively designed for Brentford F.C.!

August 1976.
Above: John Fraser gets the nod during a game of pre-season head tennis. (l-r) Steve Aylott, Bob Goldthorpe, Keith Pritchett, Gary Rolph, Danis Salman, Steve Russell, John Fraser.

2nd October 1976. Two goals from Roger Cross were not enough as Brentford, now managed by Bill Dodgin (Junior) following the resignation of John Docherty, went down 3-2 at Bradford City's Valley Parade ground.

Left: Brentford's number six, Nigel Smith, directs the traffic on the pitch.

Player/coach Ron 'Chopper' Harris caught wooing Brentford's next potential striker.

9th November 1982. Having defeated Wimbledon and Second Division Blackburn Rovers in the first two rounds of the League Cup, now renamed the Milk Cup, the Bees were drawn at home to First Division Swansea City who boasted such famous names as Ray Kennedy and Bob Latchford in their lineup. The fixture guaranteed the best Griffin Park attendance for ten years (15,262), the home fans cheered by a fine Gary Roberts strike which took the tie to a replay at Vetch Field, where goals from Roberts and Mahoney gave Brentford a deserved 2-1 win.

Right: Gary Roberts crashes in the equaliser.

1st December 1982. Brentford were rewarded for their victory over Swansea City with another First Division match-up, this time against in-form Nottingham Forest at the City Ground. Another giant killing was not on the cards, however, the home team winning 2-0 despite a spirited performance from the Bees.

Above: Paddy Roche, signed from Manchester United at the start of the season, saves at the feet of Forest skipper Ian Bowyer.

Below: Substitute Keith Bowen leaps highest to head against the post.

2nd February 1983.
Right: Daylight reveals the charred and twisted remains of the central section of the Braemar Road stand, destroyed by a fire which had quickly spread from its origin in the boiler room. The damaged section was rebuilt over the following few months, largely without the supporting columns which still characterise the remaining eastern portion of the stand.

October 1983. For the third time in two seasons, the Bees found themselves in a plum Milk Cup tie against top opposition, their 4-2 aggregate win over Charlton Athletic setting up two Second Round matches against Liverpool. In the first leg at Griffin Park, (attended by 17,859, the biggest gate since Chester visited during the 1971/72 promotion campaign) Brentford started brightly, Gary Roberts equalising a minute after Ian Rush's fortunate opener, but the team tired and lost the game 1-4, before crashing to a 4-0 second leg defeat at Anfield.

Right: Francis Joseph (number 8) receives his teammates' congratulations for the pass which set up Gary Roberts' goal at Griffin Park.

Far right: Terry Bullivant and Graham Wilkins in a race for the ball at Anfield with the Reds' Michael Robinson.

Far left: Manager Steve Perryman shows no emotion as he surveys the on-field action.

Above: The City fans can't believe it, but Gary Blissett can; he's just scored Brentford's third!

Left: Exhausted but ecstatic, Terry Evans is chaired from the pitch by elated fans.

potential giantkilling were high on the agenda as Manchester City, riding high at the top of Division Two, rolled into town for the Fourth Round tie on January 28th 1989. Clearly unhappy on the muddy pitch, City were overwhelmed as Gary Blissett (2) and Keith Jones fired the bullets that upset the apple cart and deflated the bananas of the Mancunians present in the all-ticket crowd of 12,100, powering the Bees into the last sixteen of the competition.

Unbelievably, Brentford once more missed out on top flight opposition, and were again drawn to play away from home, this time against Blackburn Rovers. The Bees had already been knocked out of the Littlewoods Cup by the Lancastrians, but with memories of the spirited 4-3 second leg win still fresh in their minds, the squad must have been more than hopeful of attaining a positive result. And so it proved to be:

"Over 3,000 Brentford supporters travelled to Ewood Park last Saturday to cheer on their favourites on to the Fifth Round of the FA Cup for the first time for forty years. Brentford's success stems from teamwork and commitment, and lanky striker Gary Blissett gave an encore performance of his two-goal show against Manchester City. Only two of Blissett's ten goals have come in Third Division games, but the Brentford supporters who gave their team tremendous encouragement around the ground, and were simply ecstatic at the final whistle, were not interested in those kind of statistics.

Left: Andy Feeley in a touchline chase for possession.

Bottom left: Roger Stanislaus helps defend Tony Parks' goal.

Bottom right: Party time in the visitors end as Big Tel is congratulated by Steve Perryman.

"Brentford, with skipper Keith Jones reinstated after a two match suspension, and giving an inspired performance in midfield, preferred the defensive style of recent signing Simon Ratcliffe to the attacking flair of Allan Cockram, and it paid handsome dividends. As manager Steve Perryman explained, "The lads carried out my instructions perfectly, and the players' commitment and supporters' encouragement saw us through. Our fans sensed midway through the second half that we could win the match at the first attempt and their encouragement provided the impetus to press forward and clinch it."

"The Bees got away to a good start in the first half with Ratcliffe, Millen and Blissett all coming close. Tony Parks was rarely alerted until making a couple of fine goaline saves early in the second period. Brentford's strength and perseverance paid off when, ten minutes from time, Richard Cadette weaved his way through to present Blissett with a chance to thump the ball high into the net. Cadette was immediately substituted by Kevin Godfrey, but three minutes later the rampant Bees capitalised on a poor back pass and Blissett, although the ball was running away from goal, prodded inside the post from a narrow angle.

"While his team joined up with their fans following the triumph,...Perryman preferred to watch them enjoying themselves from a distance, saying "It is their day. They deserve the adulation for a great performance. I want them to enjoy it to the full."

(Middlesex Chronicle, 23rd February 1989)

Into the last eight and set to lock horns with Liverpool at Anfield, the national press gave the Club the kind of coverage that their endeavours had deserved, while in the town itself tickets for the big match were snapped up in double quick time. In the event the Bees were well beaten 4-0 by a Liverpool side at the peak of their domination of the English game, but the players and fans alike received a warm ovation from all those present:

"Nearly 7,000 noisy Brentford fans held an unforgettable FA Cup quarter final party at Anfield, with a seething mass of blow up panthers and skeletons the fancy dress. But there was certainly nothing lifeless about Brentford's display in one of the world's most imposing stadiums, despite the 4-0 scoreline in mighty Liverpool's favour. From the outset Brentford's eleven heroes had the audacity to force the League champions' £8 million side back into their own half with slick one-touch football. Even the legendary Kop was silent as chants of 'Brentford' echoed round the normally fiercely partisan bastion of British soccer.

"On nine minutes the west London heroes almost did the unthinkable and score. Andy Sinton outpaced two Liverpool defenders to thread a superb ball through to the lively Richard Cadette, who beat Bruce Grobbelaar and the post by inches. That was just the filip the Bees needed, and banished any fear manager Steve Perryman had about his players freezing on their big day.

"But on fifteen minutes Liverpool took the lead, Ray Houghton's cross-cum-shot carving open the back-pedalling defence for a surprised Steve McMahon to head home inches from the floor. The setback only fuelled the resolve of the Bees' players and fans though, as the Cup giantkillers surged forward in search of an equaliser, and a magnificent midfield display took the game to Liverpool, forcing the home side's rearguard action into sometimes desperate defending. Keith Jones covered every square inch of the famous pitch, while Cockram's measured passing game found the Reds back four wanting.

"With the Bees' back four pushing forward to support their front men, an equaliser looked possible...until the 65th minute. Then John Barnes produced the sort of football Brentford's fans wished he would save for England, picking up the ball on the half way line and shimmying past Feeley and Evans to unleash an unstoppable shot past Tony Parks.

"The Kop raised a cheer of relief, followed by a healthy applause for their rival fans who rose as one to take their support to new peaks. But after the second strike, brave Brentford found themselves struggling to cope with the class of Beardsley and Barnes. In the 79th, Beardsley accepted a Houghton pass to fire home a cross shot from the left of the area, and two minutes later did the same from a John Barnes pass. But with every goal against the fervour of the travelling fans grew, forcing their side forward in search of a consolation.

"As the final whistle blew the exhausted Bees players trooped towards their jubilant fans who stood as one to salute a display which for sixty minutes matched anything Europe's best could offer."

(*Middlesex Chronicle, 22nd March 1989*)

Top: Pre-match bravado from the Brentford fans.
Above: The Anfield burgers take effect.
Top right: The Hanwell Boys replete with inflatable bees.
Below: Gary Ablett prepares to take the full force of a venomous Allan Cockram drive.
Bottom right: (l-r) Godfrey, Cadette, Millen, Stanislaus and Evans defend their goal before an open-mouthed Kop.

23rd March 1991. While remaining quite secure in defence, Brentford's main concern during the 1990/91 season had been their lack of goals, with both Holdsworth and Blissett failing to find the net with any regularity. It therefore came as quite a shock to the 5,601 fans in Griffin Park when the Bees, trailing 0-1 to Bradford City after 25 minutes, let rip with a goal bonanza, scoring four times before half-time and twice in the second period to enjoy a resounding 6-1 victory.

Above: Richard Cadette jumps to head home number five.
Right: Marcus Gayle leaves the Bradford midfield for dead seconds before smashing home the Bees' sixth of the afternoon.

Another close shave for Tranmere as Gary Blissett comes close to scoring at Prenton Park.

Disappointed, but not downhearted, the ever-popular Terry Evans is commiserated by travelling Brentford fans.

17th August 1991. After coming so close to promotion the previous year, both squad and supporters had heightened expectations about the Bees' chances of taking their place in the new First Division at the start of the 1992/93 season. Brentford's antics on the opening day of the season, a stirring 4-3 defeat of Leyton Orient, confirmed this new found optimism, while hat-trick hero Dean Holdsworth gave notice of an astonishing goal feast to come.

Right: Richard Cadette commands the attention of the Orient defence.

28th September 1991. Having rediscovered their free-scoring potential with ten goals in the previous three games, Brentford scored another three to deservedly beat Bolton Wanderers by the odd goal and move up to third place in the division.

Below: Neil Smillie congratulates Marcus Gayle, the scorer of Brentford's second.

5th October 1991.

A Terry Evans header gave Brentford all three points in the local derby at Craven Cottage, and the Bees found themselves leading the division for the first time.

Right: Neil Smillie, piling down the wing, is too quick for the Fulham defence.

22nd February 1992.

Hoping to see their team regain top spot, over 1,000 Bees fans travelled north to Stoke City's Victoria Ground for the top of the table clash, only to see the home team snatch the points with a 2-1 win.

Right: Simon Ratcliffe rushes in to help as Neil Smillie is roughly barged off the ball.

29th February 1992.

Left: A sight for sore eyes; 'Deano' in full swing and the Bees back to winning ways with an important 2-1 victory over Stockport County. The very next game (a 2-0 home win against Chester City), the prolific Holdsworth became the first Brentford player to score thirty goals in a season since Steve Phillips back in the 1977/78 promotion campaign, and eventually fell just short of equalling Jack Holliday's record 39 goals in one season for the Bees.

29th March 1992.

Above: Kevin Godfrey appears to be entertained by the pile-up in the Bournemouth penalty area as Gary Blissett and Terry Evans are caught in the clutter of bodies.

1st April 1992. Struggling to maintain their place in an automatic promotion position, Brentford travelled the short distance down the M4 to face Reading, only to suffer another disappointing away result. For many among the huge complement of Bees fans at Elm Park, the 0-0 draw was another step towards a further set of anti-climactic play-off fixtures; few predicted the awesome late run which saw the team win the next five games, leaving Brentford on the verge of promotion as the last day of the season came around.

Below: Chris Hughton (right), signed only weeks before from West Ham United, charges back to defend with Simon Ratcliffe and Keith Millen.

"Chants of 'Stockport 2 Brummies 0!' as early as the 12th minute buoyed the rampant Reds, who had 'Boro firmly under control. That was once again due to the aerial mastery of giant centre-back Terry Evans, who along with Keith Millen, restricted Posh strikers Charlery and Adcock to just a couple of long range efforts.

"With just 21 minutes to go, news filtered through on the scores of transistor radios that Bolton had taken the lead against Stoke, and that Stockport were still winning. Now the deafening chants of 'que sera sera' took on a renewed vigour - no longer were they hopeful boasts. At last the dream was within touching distance. As the seconds ticked by the Reds' supporters among the biggest Third Division gate of the day - 14,539 - were no longer happy to settle for automatic promotion...not with the title in sight.

"When referee Ashe blew the whistle on Brentford's 1991-92 campaign, unprecedented scenes of delirium swept the away end. Complete strangers hugged each other, older fans wept tears of joy, and some just stood in stunned silence as the full scale of the achievement sank in.

"The Bees heroes stood and waited to hear the other results on the halfway line - when they found out they raced towards the massed bank of fans. Lion-hearted skipper Terry Evans ripped off his shirt and threw it to the supporters before trying to scale a perimeter fence to reach them. For almost twenty minutes the Bees fans refused to budge, singing and dancing as the Peterborough fans applauded them from the pitch. Then, finally, the man who made it all possible, Phil Holder, emerged from the tunnel to punch the air in delight. The Bees were back!

(Middlesex Chronicle, 7th May 1992)

Terry Evans receives the Division Three Championship trophy back at Griffin Park.

1st September 1992. After two defeats on the trot, the Bees had picked up their first points back in Division One against Southend United, and really found their feet against a hapless Portsmouth side with a fine 4-1 victory.

Right: Gary Blissett heads home number four from close range.

Below: The Bees' Championship-winning managerial partnership of Phil 'Noddy' Holder and Wilf Rostron, pictured in happier times before Brentford's futile struggle against immediate demotion.

21st September 1992. Having defeated Fulham by an aggregate score of 4-0 in the First Round of the Coca Cola Cup, Brentford were drawn to play Tottenham Hotspur over two legs in the second round, setting up their first competitive fixture at White Hart Lane since 1949. Rather unluckily, the Bees let in two undeserved late goals to go down 1-3 in a closely fought encounter, and the quality of the Premier League side gave Spurs a 4-2 win in the second leg at Griffin Park.

Right: Detzi Kruszynski manoeuvres the ball away from the onrushing Darren Anderton.
Below: The Tottenham stewards struggle to contain the large contingent of Bees fans in the crowd of 19,365 as they celebrate Gary Blissett's equaliser with Marcus Gayle, Neil Smillie and Lee Luscombe.

17th December 1994. As if the opening-day win at Home Park was not hard enough on Plymouth, the mauling that a rampant Brentford team inflicted on the Devonians back at Griffin Park must have been too much to bear as the Bees ran amok, scoring seven times without answer against a side already striving to avoid relegation. The goal-rush was, in fact, largely unexpected; despite their excellent defensive record, Brentford had been labouring to produce a steady run of good results and were placed well away from the promotion contenders in twelfth place. This game signalled that the corner had been turned, however, and when the team next lost, twelve games later, they were sitting pretty at the top of the league.

Right: The roof of the net ripples as Robert Taylor crashes in another.
Below: Carl Hutchings and Denny Mundee congratulate Lee Harvey, scorer of Brentford's seventh.

Above: Full-back Martin 'skinhead' Grainger, not putting his foot on the ball, takes a breather.

2nd January 1995.
Left: Bright winter light at Cardiff City's Ninian Park illuminates Martin Grainger, Jamie Bates and a high-flying Kevin Dearden, as the Bees found the net another three times to win by the odd goal.

11th February 1995. The Bees made it ten goals in two home matches, an enthralling 4-3 defeat of Bradford coming a fortnight after the 6-0 rout of Cambridge United, who were made to pay dearly for eliminating Brentford from the FA Cup in an ill-tempered match back in November. 3-2 down against the Bantams with barely fifteen minutes left on the clock, the Bees sent their fans wild with a late comeback, Robert Taylor scoring from the penalty spot and Nick Forster poking in a last-gasp winner.

Top: Take your partners...for the Bees celebration twist with (l-r) Carl Hutchings, the scorer Denny Mundee, Nick Forster and Robert Taylor. Above: Fans on the Ealing Road about to jump for joy as Nicky Forster's shot creeps into the side of the net.

Right: Stan Bowles, dragged out of the pub to pass on some of his maverick skills to the young Brentford squad, photographed during a training session alongside former QPR team-mate David Webb.

4th March 1995. After their first defeat in fourteen matches the previous week at Shrewsbury, Webb's wonders put matters right with a convincing win over an always impressive Crewe Alexandra. Another large posse of Premier League scouts had come to watch Brentford's strikers in action, but it was Denny Mundee who seized the spotlight when his ninth minute drive exploded into the top right-hand corner of Crewe's net. All three points were secured in the final minute when Robert Taylor, sorely missed during his two-game suspension, coolly slotted home much to the pleasure of the 7,143 crowd (and one cat).

Top centre: Denny executes another perfect 'twiddle' to flummox his marker.
Top right: Bob Taylor scores.... and 'Pusskas' enjoys her fifteen seconds of fame with a late pitch invasion.

25th March 1995. Fun on the pier at Blackpool as Jamie Bates popped up to score his first goal of the season, helping the Bees on their way to their tenth away win.

Left: Martin Grainger, with ankles firmly bandaged for support, keeps his eyes on the prize.

Above: Despite the attentions of seven Brentford players in their own penalty box, it still needs Kevin Dearden, at full stretch, to make a fine save to deny Birmingham City.

8th April 1995. With the promotion race hotting up as the season neared its end, the tension was clearly showing at Oxford United's Manor Ground where the Bees gained a point from a dour struggle in warm spring weather.

Below: A hyped Paul Stephenson, who has just set up Robert Taylor's goal, is mobbed by his teammates. Above: Kevin Dearden lies prostrate, but Jamie Bates, Barry Ashby and Carl Hutchings prevent Oxford's Paul Moody from scoring as the thousands of Bees fans look on in anguish.

April 1995. Having accumulated seven of a possible nine points from the next three matches against relegation candidates Chester City, Leyton Orient and Cardiff City, the Bees found themselves back on top of the table just above their main promotion contenders Birmingham City. As a knock-on effect of the reduction in the size of the Premier League, only one team would be promoted automatically from Division Two, and with three fixtures remaining, the season was going down to the wire as Brentford travelled to St. Andrews to do battle with their rivals. A full complement of over 3,000 Bees supporters helped boost the attendance for the crunch match to 25,081 (one of the biggest Second Division gates of the season), but for all the vocal support of their fans, Brentford could not find a way through to goal and fell to two quick second-half sucker punches from the Blues' Kevin Francis. Worse was to come three days later as the Bees, playing before another five-figure gate back at Griffin Park, capitulated to a Bournemouth team in the middle of a remarkable escape act that would see them clear of trouble at the other end of the table. Where Brentford had slipped up, Birmingham had taken advantage of their game in hand to pull two points clear, but, as the team and fans made the trip to Bath to take on Bristol Rovers on an unseasonably hot early summers day, there was still the possibility of repeating history and winning the Championship at another club's ground on the final day of the season. Regrettably, it was the story of the 1957/58 season, as opposed to that of the 1991/92 season, which was to have far greater resonance; the Bees could only manage a 2-2 draw, while Birmingham, despite bogus rumours to the contrary on the away terraces at Twerton Park, were busy claiming the title at Huddersfield Town. Brentford had finished second, an automatic promotion position in any other season, but were set to suffer in the play-off lottery once again.

Above: A moment of false hope at Twerton Park; Robert Taylor heads home a powerful header from distance to put Brentford 2-1 up.

A show of reciprocal appreciation between Robert Taylor and Bees devotees at the end of the Bristol Rovers match.

May 1995. Both squad and supporters alike were determined to put the frustrations of the previous three games behind them as they went into the two-legged play-off semi finals against Huddersfield Town. The first leg, a free flowing match played out in the dramatic surroundings of the Alfred McAlpine Stadium, was played with true 'cup final' vigour. Both teams had chances to steal the victory; Huddersfield hit the inside of the post only to see Kevin Dearden dive on the rebound, while at the other end Robert Taylor scooped the ball onto the bar and over from six yards out when it seemed easier to score, but it was Brentford who must have been the happier of the two sides in taking a 1-1 draw back to their own turf. Things got even better back at Griffin Park as Martin Grainger converted an early penalty, but a dubious challenge on Bees keeper Kevin Dearden gave the Terriers' Andy Booth the opportunity to equalise before half time. Despite the vociferous efforts of the 12,000 screaming fans packed into the ground neither side could make any further breakthrough; a season's worth of effort had boiled down to a set of penalties....and in a moment of sickening irony it was captain Jamie Bates, perhaps the player most revered and respected by Bees fans, who missed Brentford's fifth and final penalty, leaving Darren Bullock to tie things up for Huddersfield and their ecstatic fans.

Top left: The Bees defend their goal in numbers at the Alfred McAlpine Stadium.

Left: The goal that nearly was. The Brentford fans are about to jump for joy, but Robert Taylor's shot clears the bar with Town's keeper Steve Francis beaten.

Top right: Martin Grainger fires home the penalty which put the Bees 2-1 up on aggregate back at Griffin Park.

Above: The tension shows on the faces of (l-r) Robert Taylor, Paul Stephenson, Simon Ratcliffe and Martin Grainger as the penalties are taken.

Right: It's all over. A pained Martin Grainger, hands on head, cannot be comforted.

Above: Brentford's much lauded 'FT Index', Nick Forster and Robert Taylor, limber up on the practice field.

2nd December 1995. Like many other teams before them, the Bees suffered a heavy hangover from their fraught play-off disappointments of the previous season, and with the team lying in a relegation position from November through to late January, much of the 1995/96 League campaign was spent battling to avert the potential of demotion to the Third Division. It was not all bad news, however, as Brentford enjoyed a relatively fruitful FA Cup run which was to take them so close to another meeting with Liverpool. Farnborough Town took the Bees to a replay in the First Round, drawing 1-1 at Griffin Park, before the Vauxhall Conference side were overwhelmed 4-0 at Cherrywood Road in a game screened live on Sky TV. The reward was a trip to Dean Court, where despite the horrendous injury sustained by the always important Brian Statham, a lone Robert Taylor goal was enough to avenge Bournemouth's 2-1 win in the same round of the competition in the 1991/92 season.

Top left: Barry Ashby (left) and Jamie Bates compete for possession.

Above: The team celebrate with their fans.

REEFER SHIPS

SHIPS

THE OCEAN PRINCESSES

NICK TOLERTON

ISBN: 978-1-877427-25-1

Set in Frutiger 10.5/13pt

Cover Design and Layout by Mark Andrews
for Willson Scott Publishing Limited
Endpapers: *The Motor Ship*
Email: design@willsonscott.biz

Cover Photograph and frontispiece Nick Tolerton

Printed in Taiwan by Sunny Young Printing Company
through Willson Scott Publishing Limited in association with
Merivale Press, Christchurch, New Zealand
Email: publish@willsonscott.biz
www.willsonscott.biz